Swimming Upstream:

A Story about Becoming Human

by

James P. McCullough, Jr.

DORRANCE
PUBLISHING CO
EST. 1920
PITTSBURGH, PENNSYLVANIA 15238

Dorrance Publishing Co
585 Alpha Drive
Pittsburgh, PA 15238
Visit our website at *www.dorrancebookstore.com*

ISBN: 978-1-6453-0156-1
eISBN: 978-1-6453-0737-2

To hell with despair
Search until you are grasped by Hope

Foreword

During my clinical internship training at the University of Michigan, Psychological Clinic I was introduced to the work of James P. McCullough, Jr., Ph.D. His book, *Treatment for Chronic Depression*, published in 2001 was an exemplar of clinically informed psychotherapy research, and I eagerly joined a study group exploring the various aspects of the Cognitive Behavioral Analysis System of Psychotherapy (CBASP). As is so often the case with enthusiastic clinical interns, the focus of our study and deliberations then were theoretical, mechanistic and skill-based. We analyzed and compared CBASP to what we knew, or thought we knew, about theories of psychotherapy and psychopathologies like depression. Those clinicians in the group who sought clinical techniques and wanted to "figure out the method" of CBASP contributed at that level and eventually found other challenges. However, a core group of us shared a deeper curiosity and a compelling desire to understand the complexities of this new treatment and the source of the clinical wisdom that underpinned its development. For us, the idea of an authentic and more transparent interaction with our patients made intuitive sense but was not part of our clinical learning or supervision at that time.

It was not until I began my postdoctoral fellowship that I contacted Dr. McCullough and asked to attend his intensive workshop in Richmond, VA. Sounding somewhat cautious about my request, and possibly testing my level of interest and clinical abilities, he asked why I wanted to get the training and what I wanted to do with CBASP. My response was immediate and somewhat urgent, *"Dr. McCullough, I am working with Vietnam veterans here, who have combat related PTSD, most of them struggling with chronic depression that goes undiagnosed, much less treated, they can't move forward in treatment, because depression is not addressed, and they are stuck in the system, and they get placed in treatment refractory groups!"* There was a long pause on the other end of the phone. All of my clinical inadequacies revealed, and my "Desired Outcome" slipping away moment by moment, I heard Jim say *"...Okay, let's see what we can do for them, can you come down in August?"* His response offered a welcoming sense of professional acceptance that felt like an arm around the shoulder. I did not realize that call would be the beginning of a valued professional mentorship and a lasting personal friendship. Over the intervening years, Jim has shared certain aspects of his life and the impact that his early development and difficult parental attachments had on his life and how it informed his clinical work; however, reading this book, I have a far greater appreciation for the devastating effect of these early experiences. I also have an increased respect for his internal perseverance to shift toward interpersonal engagement. More than once, while reading *Swimming Upstream: A Story about Becoming Human*, I reflected on my own family of origin and my internal motives in choosing clinical psychology as a profession. Most of all, I found myself intensely appreciative of Jim's hard work of self-discovery that led him toward relational engagement. As a beneficiary, I can attest that Jim's intentionality toward engagement is palpable and serves as a catalyst to bring the same attitude into my psychotherapy practice. Those who have had the good fortune to learn from Jim, come away with more than a knowledge and competence in a methodology. Jim's willingness to be authentic and interpersonally accessible changes the way we engage the people we work with, and in turn, opens a door of relational possibilities in their lives.

Jim McCullough allows us to bear witness to the damaging impact of his harsh and rejecting parents and the intergenerational influence of Southern white culture on the cusp of the Civil Rights movement. His memoir walks the reader through his emerging understanding of himself and his relational world much as we might observe a person's progress in psychotherapy. In fact, he brilliantly articulates his personal narrative in a manner that brings the reader to a clear understanding of the core aspects of his treatment for chronic depression, the *Cognitive Behavioral Analysis System of Psychotherapy.*

Although true, it is insufficient simply to say that Jim McCullough is in the vanguard of clinical psychologists ushering in the "third wave" of psychotherapies. His research and clinical work predates others in this recent trend in clinical psychology. It is also difficult to assert that CBASP fits a particular theory of psychotherapy. Jim weaves cognitive/affective developmental stages, and attachment-based theory, interpersonal and social learning theory into a model that places an authentic therapeutic relationship at the center of the intervention. In other words, CBASP is as unique as the developer. This book is a rare look into the most intimate experiences of a brilliant clinician and master psychotherapist who teaches us to strive to construct meaning and purpose out of our most painful life experiences. This process may start for each of us by the use of Jim's mantra: "*PUSH PAST INTERPERSONAL AVOIDANCE; PLUNGE INTO RELATIONSHIP; LOOK FOR AVENUES OF PERSONAL GROWTH!*" This is a great start for our desired outcomes; however, it is not a linear process and requires vigilance and honest self-reflection. Jim McCullough teaches us to have the courage to remain open and accepting of safe and loving relationships so that we can begin to learn self-compassion and gain mastery over wounds from the past as well as gain the potential to determine our own direction with anticipation of new discoveries.

Todd K. Favorite, Ph.D., ABPP
Director, University Psychological Clinic
Clinical Associate Professor, University of Michigan Medical School
U of M, Rackham Graduate School

Preface

Because of my harmful and dysfunctional early developmental beginnings, I always felt that I was swimming upstream. Nothing I did as a child, adolescent or adult has been easy. For forty-seven years after receiving a Ph.D. in 1970 in Clinical Psychology at the University of Georgia, I worked as an academic clinical psychologist in a university. The personal burdens I carried from my early years informed the trajectory of my didactic career and the form my work took. Struggling with a chronic depression disorder as an adolescent, I became interested in what early experiences contributed to depression; not surprisingly, I spent most of the time as a clinical professor conducting depression research and treating chronically depressed patients.

During the 1970s, very little was known about depression; treatment prognosis was poor for those presenting with long-term histories of dysphoria. Soon after entering the university as an assistant professor, I constructed a treatment model for this population and spent the remainder of my career developing and fine-tuning the only psychotherapy model designed to treat the chronically depressed adult. Today, the model is known as *The Cognitive Behavioral Analysis System of Psychotherapy*

(CBASP). The emphasis in the label rests on the word "analysis" because the therapy techniques identify and then remedy the causes that maintain the disorder. CBASP has been empirically tested and found effective in the United States, Germany, Switzerland, United Kingdom, the Netherlands, Finland and Sweden. As noted, CBASP is designed to treat the diagnostic group known in the American Psychiatric Association's *Diagnostic and Statistical Model of Mental Disorders-5 (2013)* as Persistent Depressive Disorder (i.e. chronic depression).

The major goals in writing this memoir are to describe the early harmful experiences which thrust me into a destructive living cycle resulting in my spending many subsequent years trying to understand and remediate the intrapersonal emotional, cognitive and behavioral damage; and secondly, to describe how I modified the destructive life trajectory and altered the direction of my life.

My memoir is divided into two parts. It is formatted in two partitions mimicking an earlier memoir published in 1959 by Viktor E. Frankl (*Man's Search for Meaning*. Beacon Press: Boston). I have reread Frankl's book perhaps a dozen times and always experienced great inspiration and hope in his words. His description of the horrific experiences in the German death camps constituted *Part One*; the development of his therapy model, Logotherapy, was described in *Part Two*. Taken together, they offered an attractive format with which to organize my own memoir. Our histories are vastly different but the organizational structure of his text fits neatly in the presentation of my life story and then, how I responded to my difficult beginnings.

Part One in my memoir describes the horrific early life-problems I faced and the origins of my chronic depression. Next, I describe several interpersonal relationships that enabled me to achieve an exodus from the destructive path I was traveling. *Part Two* presents a descriptive overview of my psychotherapy model for chronic depression (*i.e.*

Cognitive Behavioral Analysis System of Psychotherapy: CBASP) to illustrate how the salubrious encounters with helpful comrades over the years informed my construction of an interpersonal psychotherapy system to treat early-onset chronic patients. Using CBASP, I have personally treated over 450 chronically depressed patients during my clinical career of forty-seven years.

Being eighty-two years old provides a unique perspective from which to conduct a life-review. Several emotional themes have been lifelong companions: the pain of early rejection, the fears of feeling unsafe during my elementary school years, my inability to trust that significant others would protect me from harm and danger, and the overwhelming dread of living in a world where feeling alone and emotionally vulnerable have been a constant threat; taken together, these emotional themes reside in most of my early emotional memories. In my field of clinical psychology, many colleagues argue that the way we think determines our emotions. Personally, this has not been my experience. Rather, hurtful emotive memories stemming from reality-based interpersonal origins have informed my emotional life. For years, these memories remained an encrusted reality highly resistant to change. Memories of actual rejection were paramount. Trying to think differently about these events never modified the validity of these remembrances and experiences; rather, it took salubrious real-world experiences to break up and loosen this intrapersonal rejection landscape. Intrapersonal change occurred as I encountered individuals who I realized were qualitatively different from familial malevolent persons. The process of interpersonal healing and trust has been arduous and long and helped in part by the dogged persistence of those whom I realized loved me.

Before I begin to describe my early developmental history, I will make one general observation about childhood. Every child, if personal maturity is to be achieved, is unavoidably faced with intra-familial challenges that he or she must master. Families or care-giving units present tasks that a child must successfully navigate, or developmental-maturational growth in the social-interpersonal arena may be compromised; in the extreme case of chronic depression where dysfunctional experiences predominate, developmental-maturational growth is often inhibited. Looking back on my early years, I failed to master the emotional challenges presented by both parents. From my perspective, rejection and punishment were unavoidable outcomes regardless of what I did; I was caught for the first almost eighteen years in an unresolvable dilemma with no exit, to quote a play title from Jean Paul Sartre. I have paid a significant personal price for this extended captivity—chronic depression being one. The tragedy of my early history is that I never knew how to do anything other than what I did—that is, just try to survive. I perceived the early reality of my learning experiences as the way my life was meant to be. The only thing I was certain of as a young boy was that I was a failure, unlovable and incapable of succeeding at anything I did.

Contents

PART ONE:
Swimming Upstream

"People we loved broke our hearts because only they had access to them, and we broke our own hearts later by following their footsteps and reenacting their mistakes" (Mary Karr, 2015. *Art of Memoir*, New York: Harper Perennial. p. 163.) ...until...

Chapter One:

The Early Years

My parents' marriage lasted for forty-eight years. I grew up in the 1940s and 1950s in a middle-income family and lived comfortably. My father, who died when he was sixty-eight years old of cardio-vascular heart disease, worked long hours as a middle-level executive in an oil and gas corporation in Shreveport, Louisiana. Mother was professionally unemployed except for her vocation as "homemaker;" she kept the house clean, washed our clothes and cooked our meals. I was an only child for eleven years and was positioned between two individuals who were quite rigid and set in their ways. I lived in the same house for fifteen years. The house was a comfortable, two-story structure at 724 McCormick Street in Shreveport, Louisiana. During my time at home, I remained largely unaware that there was a qualitatively different world outside compared to the only world I knew with my parents. My insular view was bordered by white walls, quaint old-south pictures, frequently vacuumed rugs, squeaky-clean furniture with ashtrays (because my father smoked two-packs of Lucky Strike cigarettes daily), tablecloths spread at meals, folded cloth napkins, correctly placed silverware, rigidly held apartheid attitudes and the incessant bickering of parents, particularly at mealtime. I don't remember the content of our table-conversations; however, I do recall my father always teasing my mother about small details such as how much food or how big a slice of meat she wanted—he always served the food at our meals. In keeping with their apartheid attitudes, African Americans never came to our front door, only to the back, and calling them by their actual names was not important. Using surnames or the titles Mr. or Mrs. was explicitly prohibited. Asking why they were treated this way never occurred to me—I went along with the custom.

Did my parents love each other? I never knew and spent little time thinking about it because I was too self-involved and afraid of the world that lay outside our home. My mother often reminded me that our frequent arguments and conflicts were absent in her childhood home, and she never understood why there was so much hostility in ours. To me, these comments always meant that I was the core problem. She always reacted to the continual angry exchanges between my father and me with a passive sigh and an expression of resignation. I never recall any protest on her part concerning the way my father treated me. Her submissive behavior vis-à-vis the interpersonal war that raged between us was disheartening and left me feeling quite alone. Mother's resignation during such events also contributed to my generalized view that no one would ever take my side nor protect me from his angry assaults. Problems were always my fault and, of course, I blamed myself for the family conflicts and for the emotional chaos that characterized our home life.

My sister was born when I was eleven. The memories I have of our interactions remain vague. However, I am aware that I was not a supportive older brother—a fact that I regret to this day. When she was six, I left for college and rarely returned home.

My Father: He left a malevolent legacy on my life, but ironically I never felt I knew who he was apart from his anger. I remained ignorant concerning what he liked, who he liked or what his early developmental years were like. I never heard him say he loved my mother, nor did I ever see him caress her, hold her hands or kiss her on her mouth. The household was emotionally sterile and punitive and was, at least from my perspective, devoid of gentle care and concern for its family members; emotional memories of love and tenderness between the two of them or between them and me were absent. Our home-life always reminded me in later years of a desert without water.

Father grew up the oldest child of six siblings in Franklin, Louisiana, a rural small south Louisiana town in the 1910s. His family was always poor. The only child photograph of him I remember was one taken with his younger brother. In the picture, he was about six years-old in stripped overalls held up by suspenders and standing on a wooden front porch—the picture always reminded me of the type one sees in older, rural sections of the south where children are standing on a bare white-washed front porch with 4x4s holding up the roof. In the photograph, he wasn't wearing shoes—shoes were prized in his household, and there were times when siblings had to share their shoes. Family lore describes his father as a person who could never hold a job, so the family always struggled for money to put enough food on the table. From what I've pieced together, based on the sparse information I have, he raised me with the same anger and rejection that characterized his relationship with his father. My suspicions were confirmed over thirty years ago while talking with his younger sister. She asked, and I disclosed, what growing up around my father was like. She was the only family member in that Franklin clan with whom I shared my early experiences. After listening to my story, she exclaimed that this was exactly the way my father had been raised—frequent punishment, severe criticism and incessant verbal abuse by the 'ole man.' My aunt's name was Florence but everyone called her Shoo. As a little girl, so the story goes, whenever she stood near my grandfather, he would exclaim with gestures, "Shoo, shoo!" The label stuck.

This conversation with Shoo was confirmation that my early memories were valid and largely correct. I wrote a poem following the second conversation I had with Shoo. I was fifty-one years old at the time.

> You stepped out and spoke to me,
> Your words were like cool water
> Given to lips that had been parched
> For a long time by rays from a hot sun,
> And for a while I understood and could see.
>
> Then, the vision became too painful,
> You returned to the ground
> From which you had become figure,
> I turned away and tried to forget
> The memory of our touch disdainful.
>
> Then you came again, reaching out in cheer,
> This time I didn't turn away,
> Your love and understanding
> Once more a soothing balm that
> Prodded me to reach out, damn the fear.

Unlike his father, mine worked hard, was impeccably conscientious and was characterized by all as honest. After dropping out his final year in mechanical engineering at Louisiana State University, he had to go to work to financially support his mother and family for eight years, fulfilling the role of the oldest child. Since my father rarely talked about his father or his early years, I had few sources describing his history except for a few conversations and letters from his siblings. I knew and know very little about him.

As a child, we infrequently visited his family in south Louisiana. Some of what I did learn, in spite of his general laconic reticence, came from his disclosure of how brutal the fathers in his family were with their sons. He seemed rather proud to talk about this autobiographical aspect of his history. His family stories extended back five generations—to civil-war times. One traumatic tale concerned the way he learned to swim. In south Louisiana, there are deep bayous (creeks) in the countryside and one afternoon he was walking with his uncle. They crossed a wooden bridge built over a wide and deep bayou. His uncle asked if he knew how to swim. He didn't. The older man said he'd teach him. He picked him up by the back of his britches and threw him in the middle of the water. "Now swim!" Somehow, my father made it to the bank with no help. His uncle acted throughout as if his struggles and cries for help were humorous. He later commented that he never knew if the older man would have pulled him out had he not been able to reach the bank. The general theme of the type of harsh brutality in this story and others like it and the total lack of nurture and support fathers extended to their sons was obviously repeated over generations. He lived out the fifth generation with me.

As noted above, another family story involved his being forced to quit Louisiana State University after three years when his family's financial needs drained his available college money. He never completed a B.S. mechanical engineering degree at Louisiana State University; instead, he returned home to support his family of nine. He and my mother married in 1932 and moved to Baton Rouge, Louisiana; I was born four years later. I recall a workaholic father who labored long hours in a north Louisiana oil and natural gas corporation during the 1940s, 1950s and 1960s. He finished his career as a middle executive in the United Gas Pipe Line Company in Shreveport and as head of the oil and gas contract purchasing department—I always opined this was a significant achievement for a man with his rural background and harsh upbringing, especially one who had grown up poor during the depression era. As an adult, he did make sufficient money that allowed his family to live well and that supported two children through college. Another significant consequence of his work was that I had enough financial support to leave home, and with the degrees of freedom that accrued with these financial benefits, I finally broke free of the malevolent generational interaction trajectory between sons and fathers in the McCullough clan. This fact has been one of the major accomplishments of my life. I stopped the sixth generation of abuse between fathers and sons in my family when my wife and I had our first child.

Most activities that characterized my early family life ended up being major hassles because of some conflict between him and me—and, as usual, at such times my mother always played the quiet, passive role. Once or twice a year the three of us would drive 350 miles to Memphis, Tennessee where my mother's family lived. My dad would drive our 1940 four-door Plymouth on eighteen-foot two-lane highways to visit her relatives. Before leaving our driveway, he would be angry with something I had done packing my clothes or carrying suitcases to the car. I always did something he didn't like and an argument would ensue. By the time we left the driveway, I wanted to stay home. I rode in the back seat and can still see the back of his head as he drove our Plymouth down the highway. He would always show me the redness of his hands when we arrived, telling me how hard he had gripped the steering wheel during the eight-hour trip. I also remember wondering on these extended drives why I couldn't do anything right and why everything always seemed to go wrong between us. He would drive in silence for many miles, and my mother never said anything. I sat quietly during these periods, judging myself to be the major family problem—my thoughts usually drifted to wishing I was dead.

Once, he took me on a deep-sea fishing trip on a charter boat in Fort Walton Beach, Florida. I was about ten years old at the time. It was a large boat where people lined the rails on both the port and starboard sides and dropped baited hand-held lines in the water at a signal from a loud, clanging bell. Each line had multiple hooks with a heavy weight at the end and the captain warned everyone to drop our lines overboard and not throw them from the boat. Of course, I tried to throw my line and two of my hooks dug in at the back of my hand and the pull of the heavy weight opened up deep gashes across the length of my left palm. Of course, my father lost his temper and loudly chastised me in front of the captain and the adults standing nearby. All the while, I was trying to stem the blood flow that by this time was soaking my shirt and pants. I don't remember who, but someone wrapped my hand with gauze, and I remained on board holding my hand and sitting on a bench along the inner-wall until the trip was over. My mother was waiting for us when we exited the boat, and he started in again with another lecture on how I was nothing but a screw-up who never did anything right. Once again, a family outing had turned into a nightmare and it was my fault. Always, always, I had messed up and ruined what promised to be an enjoyable day of fishing. Another destructive conclusion I drew was that I was ruining my father's life—he would be okay if I were not around. Little did I realize at this stage of my life that my father was a child trying to raise a child.

My earliest memory of him occurred when I was about four or five years old. A mechanical engineer by training, he spent much of his spare time at home in his workshop in our one-car garage. He worked with wood and metal, constructing furniture items and repairing things around the house. One day in his workshop, I was trying to drive a large nail into a piece of wood with a hammer. I wasn't having much success. He looked at me and exclaimed disgustedly, and I can still smell the sawdust of his workshop when he said something like, "You can't do anything right! Anyone can hammer a nail in wood." This experience set a tone for our relationship which continued for as long as I can remember. I was not sorry when he died in 1968. I cannot remember one positive remark he ever made about anything I ever did. What he did contribute to me was to teach me a self-awareness of perceived failure, feelings of inadequacy and a generalized interpersonal distrust.

When I was a young lad about nine, I was bathing in the tub one morning while he was shaving. I innocently mentioned that I had rubbed my genitals and it had felt good. He stopped shaving and turned on me abruptly. In a loud voice, he commanded that I must never touch myself again! I was terrified and remember the cold fear that ran up and down my spine. I remember that cold emotional feeling as if it were yesterday. Little did I realize at the time what effect that brief innocuous interaction would have on my life. Sometimes he would inquire menacingly if I had touched myself lately (he never said penis), and, of course, I vehemently denied it—one of many lies I learned to tell. Concluding that good people don't do the things that I kept on doing, such as fondling my penis, I concluded that I was not one of these good people. The saliency of this memory remained because of the fear that was associated with my emergent sexuality. The early fear took years to extinguish and my penis remained a constant source of shame; concomitantly, I interpreted as weakness my inability to inhibit fondling my penis and this self-view haunted me for years. Sometimes when I pictured myself and what I looked like, the mental image was void of a penis. As I pen this memory, the bathroom incident seems rather trivial. But to me it was a life-changing event that occurred at a very early age. Most adolescent boys who are well-adjusted feel proud of their genitals. This was not my lot, and like so many other fears, I paid an exorbitant price for this exchange during my teenage years and beyond. Later, when a freshman at Louisiana State University, I was asked a question during a fraternity initiation—I was eighteen at the time. I had been placed in a wooden coffin with the brothers standing around. Asked if I ever "jacked off," I once again said vehemently, "NO!" Of course, my words were met with hoots and howls, but the early childhood experience with my father was still salient and was reiterated once again as a university freshman. Remembering that time, I felt I had done the right thing by doing the exact thing I had done all my life—that is, denying that I had a penis.

I went through the eighth and ninth grades in junior high school frightened and feeling inadequate. Distinct memories of feeling that I was "bad" and that something was terribly wrong with me followed my steps through the halls of middle school. I had no understanding of what was wrong. Peer relationships were not healthy as I waited for the next shoe to fall and label me as a misfit. I passed my courses but misbehaved in class and was often called out and sent to the principal's office. Falling into one malevolent situation after another, I'm certain the faculty was relieved to see me move on to high school.

At fourteen years old, I remember riding a Cushman motor scooter as did the majority of my peers in the school. My carburetor went bad and during a lunch break, I went to the parking lot where the scooters were parked and stole a carburetor from a newer cycle. I was never caught nor did I realize it at the time, but had I been apprehended, my life would have taken a severe turn on a road that might have been one with no return—that road being entrance into the legal penal system for juveniles.

I've often wondered why I seemed to stay in trouble, and, as an adult who has raised three children, I now know why. Staying in trouble was all I had learned in my punitive home-schooling environment. I had been taught well to live as I did by two parents who, I am convinced now, were well-meaning. They didn't set out to put me on a rejection–punishment trajectory, but as we function as adults with what we learn as children, I became the recipient of a toxic lesson plan—do as you have been taught—misbehave.

Ironically, my mother frequently told me that I was much loved, especially by my father. Honestly, I never felt loved and the feeling of being loved had to be experienced much later before I even understood what the *love* word meant. What I did experience was a feeling of pressure similar to the pressure-cooker my mother used to cook vegetables. When she cooked with it, the pot continually gave off a jet of steam from a metal cap on the top to relieve the pressure inside. I remember this sense of pressure, of being compressed by others and felt it at school, in church, with my friends and of course the entire time I was living at home. This pressure experience haunted me for years and was present in social relationships I had—particularly with girls. I called it the 'wind-tunnel' feeling and it afforded no calm. I also remember thinking during early adolescence that something was really wrong with my brain as I had little or no control over my life or emotions. I deserved nothing good. I was a *bad seed*.

As mentioned, I ran afoul of my junior high school teachers and the administration because of many discipline violations. I once threw a rotten tomato into a crowd of girls standing in the back of the school gym. At the end of each gym period, the boys and girls congregated in a group and entered through different doors. I can still see Anne Willis, the victim, whom I hit with the tomato; shortly afterwards, the principal brought Anne to my class and called me to come with them. Anne was still wearing the white gym blouse with the tomato stains all down the front. I had to personally apologize to Anne for my misdeed, and, once more, my parents were called and I got school detention for a week. During these years, my father, on a regular basis, would lecture me almost nightly about what a "loser I was." These blistering verbiages occurred after I was in bed and lying on top of the sheets. He would enter my bedroom and the tirade would begin. They continued for long periods, and again, my mother would remain passively quiet downstairs in the kitchen—the farthest point from my bedroom. As usual, my father would remind me repeatedly how I had ruined the family. I can still picture him holding onto both posts on the bed while he talked. Why he didn't break the posts, I'll never understand. His rants continued, I guess, until he couldn't think of anything else negative to say. When he left, I remember feeling so physically weak that I could barely turn over in bed. Years after these lectures, these memories remained, and during difficult periods in my life, I could still hear his voice and would not be able to shut off his condemning accusations in my head. During these times of despair, it felt as if the rejection emotions had no bottom— they were limitless.

Father was a bright individual intellectually but the angriest man I ever knew. We never wrestled or touched physically that I can recall and whenever he physically bumped into me, it was always inadvertent; he would draw in his breath with a hissing sound like he had done something wrong. Another clear emotional memory I have is that I never felt that he really liked or respected women—at least he never talked like he did. He laughed at the foibles of his secretaries, women drivers were the butt of his jokes, and he joked about the mannerisms of females he knew in church. And of course, there was the incessant teasing of my mother. Another remembered verbal mannerism of his occurred when I asked questions he didn't want to answer. His stock reaction was, "Ne'r mind." Such were his comments when I tried to tell him what I was doing, or when I needed advice or just wanted to talk—"Ne'r mind," "Ne'r mind," "Ne'r mind," "Ne'r mind."...ad infinitum.

Whenever my parents invited friends over for a visit, the events had a defining feature. I listened to many of these conversations sitting on our stairs and out of sight of the adults sitting in the living room. These conversations involved the constant passage of facts, and as I recall, there was almost a total absence of expressed emotionality. After the guests left, I would deliberately try to recall what had been said; regardless of how hard I tried, I couldn't remember much of what had been said—even though these visits lasted for several hours. This myriad flow of words without emotion later reminded me of Jean Paul Sartre's description of his first ten years in his memoir, *Les Mots*—his recollections of these years were nothing but a stream of words, a paucity of affect, hollow facts and emptiness.

The upshot of these early memories left me with one burning question: WHY? Why me? Why did I have a family like this? I have three children all of whom are now in their 40s. I never knew why I had been treated the way I had, but the one thought I had always in adulthood was never to treat my children the way I had been treated. It took an enormous effort on my part to break the generational legacy of abuse between fathers and sons because it was all I knew from my earlier experiences—hostility when things didn't go the way I wanted, impatience, little to no knowledge about teaching my children how to manage their impulses and learning to control their emotions, a lack of knowing how to teach through encouraging positive behavior, and how to use their mistakes to teach more appropriate behaviors.

I finally concluded that answering the WHY question as to the reasons my father treated me as he did was impossible. Too many pieces in his past are missing for me and because he was never interested in understanding his past, it was a closed book. His modus operandi as a father was to do the only thing he learned and just pass it on. I walked on eggshells around him most of my life never knowing whether to run away or stay. I never learned how to solve problems—with myself or with other people. I never learned how to do anything but keep my distance from him interpersonally and avoid closeness that angered him. This strategy generalized to other people around whom I lived. I never knew warmth or safety. Attitudinally, I assumed immediately that if anything went wrong, it was my fault. I entered young adulthood with deep interpersonal fears while maintaining a safe interpersonal distance from others.

How would I summarily describe this man who grew up in a primitive environment in south Louisiana? He was frightening to me because of his hostile-dominant demeanor, and the most damning part is that I never knew who he really was or what drove him to behave as he did. Not knowing who he was made it very difficult for me to define who I was. Describing my father is best done with two words—*angry* and *detached*. Ironically, this angry and interpersonally detached individual behaved in a friendly manner with other people. His conduct here was always confusing to me. Outside our relationship, he appeared to be well liked and to get along with others. This was in Shreveport, Louisiana during the 1940s, 1950s and 1960s, and his friends included work colleagues, social visitors, and church members in our large First Methodist Church, where he taught Sunday classes and served in administrative capacities. He seemed to be regarded positively and, as best as I can recall, appeared to be respected in the community. Having described his social persona as an outgoing friendly demeanor, I never knew anything he liked—only what he did not—and I opined that I was always high on that list. I don't remember ever feeling that he would take care of me nor did I ever feel he loved me. No one outside my family had any idea what was happening between the two us. This explained the surprised reactions I would get from friends whenever I disclosed what it was like growing up with him.

I realized only much later that adults must teach a child how to control their emotions. While living in my household, I could not control my anger and I fought back with my father. Once again I interpreted my continual rage and generalized anger toward him, my mother, teachers, peers, and most people I met as weakness on my part—I was just a *bad seed*.

Nothing I ever did in my family alleviated the interpersonal conditions I grew up with. This was true between my parents and me until both died. It was always the same—repetitive failure, interpersonal avoidance, gross skill deficits and my lack of trust in both of them. As I look back on these early years, I was trapped with two caretakers and had no way to end the all-encompassing negativity.

According to the Austro-Hungarian thinker, Karl Polanyi, my perceptions of reality then comprised two dimensions: *tacit experiences* (out of awareness) and the *explicit* domain (awareness memories & experiences). However, I realized later that the tacit experiences, of which I was not aware, had a direct bearing on my emotions and behavior. I've spent a lifetime continually discovering these tacit memories. One occurred recently while I was studying an on-line course for professional licensure credentialing credits. I was filled with dread, thinking I would surely fail. This type of knee jerk response has always been associated with classroom didactics stemming from early elementary school experiences. In spite of the self-doubts, I plowed ahead with the course and passed it for certification.

Polanyi also defined a second perceptual level which he labeled the *explicit* domain that denoted memories and meaning structures of which I *was* aware and that I drew from directly. Every time I sit in a committee meeting with a male chairperson, my first associations are negative expectancies that nothing good will come of my participation. Emotive memories of numerous experiences I had with my father were the tacit and explicit lenses through which I organized reality, usually in self-destructive ways—repetitive failure due to gross skill deficits, interpersonal avoidance, and my lack of trust in anyone.

The emotional state of my destructive learning while at home remained consistent until I finally left the family at age eighteen. I took these tacit and explicit life-lessons, emotional memories and interpersonal expectancies, now hard-wired at all levels in my brain, and barely managed to graduate from Louisiana State University four years later with a C+ average. The essential reason I didn't quit the university was the very real fact that there was nowhere else to go; there was nothing to return to—no place offered any relief from the emotional chaos and despair. I was an adult in chronological age, but emotionally and cognitively, I functioned at a childlike level, acting and emoting as I did at a much earlier age. I didn't know how to relate to others, and I was interpersonally isolated—feeling very much alone. What is ironic and what has characterized me throughout my life has been a veneer of sociability, which allowed me to maintain some semblance of normalcy with fraternity brothers and friends around whom I lived. I've often wondered why I didn't take my life at this point. Deep down inside, I've always felt there had to be a better way to live. Where this feeling came from is unknown. I saw fraternity brothers happy, and I had memories of visiting other high school friends' homes where positive interactions occurred. I also knew of a few peers who had good relationships with their fathers. Maybe these memories provided a healthy crack-in-the-door view of what might be possible; however, I had no idea how to actualize it. This deep hope never left my soul, though it took years to achieve that dream. In summary, looking back at this period in my life, I can best describe it as a circular, self-destructive orbit where today was only a replay of yesterday and tomorrow offered only more of the same.

My Mother: Years after I married Rosemary, and I have been married for fifty-five years, I would wake up during the night and look at my wife sleeping softly by my side. My reaction would be to think to myself while concomitantly breathing a sigh of relief, "Thank God Rosie is *not* my mother." Some years ago, I wrote a poem during a particularly difficult and disappointing period in my academic career when I very much needed collegial support and didn't get it. The occasion reminded me of the times, many years before, when I felt very isolated and distressed in the presence of my mother.

Mother was not a gentle person,
Never held me or softly patted my arm,
She was not reassuring nor did she bring calm.

To her, it was important how things looked -
to others,
She clung to the surface, did not offer affection
Was absent when I needed protection.

From her I learned manners and to be polite,
The empty heart to her was unknown
Known were dutiful routines - I remained alone.

She never knew me,
The one who came from between her legs,
The one she bore from a fertilized egg.

Tragedy, tragic with my mother's liaison
We passed in the night
I've paid an exorbitant price for her oversight.

The Memphis Clan. Mother came from Memphis, Tennessee and was born into a very religious Methodist family who lived at 3605 Carnes Avenue. Her father owned a large quantity of land but lost it by default during the Depression. Unable to meet his land-tax burden, his estate had to be sold. However, before the financial forfeiture, he contributed significant funds to build St. Luke's Methodist Church on Highlands Avenue which attracted a large membership during my childhood years. Our family attended services there in the summer when we visited the grandparents. We stayed in their rambling house, and I spent those warm summer nights on "the sleeping porch." There was no air-conditioning and the windows remained open. The roar of crickets in the trees and other sounds of the night were soothing to me as I lay in bed.

My mother, like her mother, was a constant bundle of activity. We called my grandmother, BaGa. I recall little about my grandfather nor did Mother say much about him. What's strange to me is how one can live with people for years and not talk about who they were—sharing cherished memories, good and bad, talk about the significant events that influenced their lives, describe how they expressed love within and outside the family, discuss their favorite activities and what they liked and didn't like to do, implicate essential values that were important to them, and share what their dreams and goals were, etc. She did talk some about some members of her family but rarely spoke about her father. However, Mother's family was unlike my father's. They were not financially poor and obvious love and affection were present. Still, there was great silence about my grandfather. One uncle, Chussy, who was my mother's brother and whom I will discuss later, once told me that he had very few conversations with his dad; thus, I grew up with little to no knowledge about both parents' childhood experiences with their fathers. The previous male generation of fathers in my family remained a mystery.

I did learn several things about this Methodist Memphis clan. One, Abraham Lincoln was hated, and in my great-grandmother's house, his name could not be spoken. The remnants of the Ole South were very much present in the Memphis group and apartheid was clearly important to the adults. Moral rigidity characterized the household. For example, alcohol was anathema and no one, to my knowledge, drank; in addition, movie-going on Sundays was frowned upon and no dancing was allowed on the Sabbath. I never achieved a clear appreciation of masculine functioning from the men who lived in Memphis. As noted, my grandfather remained a shadowy figure, though I always heard he was a very good and religious man. He and my grandmother from what I heard (but never observed) appeared to have a loving marriage. When he died in the early 1940's, Mother remarked that her mother withdrew into a severe depression for several years.

Both of my uncles were World War II veterans and lived with their families close to the home-place on Carnes Avenue. One, Uncle Rad, was a Marine who saw the worst of the Great War as a forward observer in the Pacific Theater. I do know from our family lore that he and his comrades went island hopping (Philippines, Tinian, Iwo Jima, Saipan, etc.) with mainland Japan being the ultimate goal. The invasion of Japan never occurred because the war ended after the Atomic Bomb was dropped on Hiroshima and Nagasaki. Rad would never discuss his grizzly experiences with me (though I would have loved to have heard about them and how he survived). He followed the family tradition with silence about his past.

My other uncle, Chussy, was in the Air Force and stationed in North Africa. He was in the Quartermaster Corp and assigned to a unit in North Africa which unloaded and constructed boxed-up P-38 airplanes with their twin fuselages, twin tails and dual props. I always loved P-38 fighters because of their sleek design and fire power. I once tacked a picture of a P-38 to my bedroom wall in Shreveport. This uncle, Chussy as we called him, taught me how to play golf when I was around ten years-old. He had some old clubs in my grandparents' basement that he used as a boy, and he gave his old set to me—a driver, niblick, driving iron, mid-mashie, mashie iron, and putter. Chussy was an excellent one-handicap golfer who played with Wilson irons and shot his age at sixty-eight. His old putter now hangs on my office wall alongside his red 1-wood cover. Three of my fondest childhood memories involve Chussy: (1) trying hard to master the golf swing with his mentoring and feedback; and (2) shooting a seventy-two when we played our last round together at Galloway Golf Course in Memphis some thirty years ago. I had had the good fortune of playing the Old Course at St. Andrews (the home of golf in Scotland), and (3) right before Chussy died, I gave him an Old Course scorecard, black tee bag and ball with the Old Course's logos on them, and a turf of grass from the hallowed first tee. His joy over the gift was evident. To a knowledgeable golfer, St. Andrews is the Holy Grail of golf.

Outside my experiences with Chussy, the emotional impressions of my mother's side of the family was that it was predominantly a matriarchy. Women were dominant and the males were generally passive, strove to be good Christians and held their testosterone in check. I rarely saw my uncle Radford kiss or caress his wife, and, not surprisingly, there was no affection expressed between my father and mother while we were in Memphis. There was one exception. I always felt that Chussy and his wife, Helen, had the best marriage in the family. I saw the two of them kiss and caress frequently. As often as possible during our visits to Memphis, I would walk to their house on 410 Alexander Street, immensely enjoying the visits there. At the time, I didn't think much about why I found their loving oasis such a relief. I now know why I sought them out. Comparing the sterile interpersonal interactions that reigned in the rest of the family, Chussy and Helen's relationship always stood out in stark contrast.

As a general rule, obscene language among the males in my mother's family was frowned upon, alcohol was absent, going to church and singing in the choir were prominent, and the male interactions, outside of my relationship with Chussy, largely remained shadowy. My lucid memories involve the interactions of the women, particularly my mother, her sister, my uncles' wives and grandmother. They talked about shopping, maintaining the house, teaching school (one aunt was a teacher), family matters and religious and moral topics. My mother had one sister and her husband was in the Coast Guard and was a master carpenter. He died of a myocardial infarction when I was six. Ironically, my relationship with my father was a bit calmer during the periods when we visited my grandparents. However, consistent with the theme of these years, my grandmother often told me that I must behave myself when I returned home because I was causing undue strain on my mother. Once again, I was reminded of my bad-boy role and as the one who always personified the "family problem." Even in Memphis, I couldn't escape the guilt role of being the problem child, a self-fulfilling prophecy if ever there was one.

Back in Shreveport. One of my earliest memories of Mother was a dinner occasion when I failed to eat everything on my plate. She was a "stickler" for table rules—polite etiquette in our house required that one eat everything on his or her plate. It was irrelevant that I might not like some food or beverage and not want to partake. The rule applied to the meal I was served. I always hated split-pea soup and during one meal, split-pea soup was placed in a bowl at my place. I refused to eat it. Still sitting at the table with the soup uneaten at midnight, long after my parents had gone to bed, I made the critical decision. I tip-toed into the bathroom and threw the soup in the toilet. The next morning I swore to my mother that I had eaten the soup. She said nothing more about the incident.

I cannot remember ever being soothed by her presence or calmed by her touch. She was interpersonally very cold and detached and an extremely rational individual about life's issues and problems.

The subtleties of the emotional learning between a child and adult remain tacit (unknown) knowledge until the child grows up. Such was the case with me. I didn't realize that the emotional desert I experienced daily with my mother was to have such an impact on my later life—it was just the way life was and I assumed that everyone experienced the same from their mothers. The effects of my maternal relationship were pervasive in my life and disastrous throughout the first half of my life. I found myself emotionally caught between two parents who positioned me in the middle and they never seemed to know what to do with me except punish and criticize. When I was little, my mother would read me childhood stories that included themes about male and female animals. She would emphasize the fact that animal mothers frequently had to protect their babies from the fathers who would try to harm them. These stories made an indelible impression upon me that lasted for years. I don't think she was really aware of the message she was sending, that being: *my personal world was unsafe, and I should stay close to her.* I took her message to heart and did remain close. These feelings remained diffuse. As I recall them now, I realize that they were symbiotically connected with sexual emotional overtones that concomitantly evoked a strong fear of being separated from my mother comingled with feelings of inadequacy and failure. I was afraid of my mother on one hand and simultaneously drawn to her with promises of safety and security that never fully materialized. My father often railed against my mother for the way she acted toward me with her excessive attentions and over-protective behavior - he never did anything about it but fuss and fume. He was angered by the attentions I was receiving and this was to remain a long-standing source of contention between the two of them. I was emotionally caught in the middle between both and had no idea how to extract myself from this conflictual middle-position. I found myself emotionally confused, pulled in two directions between the two of them and caught in a no-win situation.

I've said earlier that my mother never intervened when my father was verbally blistering me; rather, she would often sigh in despair that her home life was never like ours. She found other ways to intervene with subtle emotional messages that entrapped me. For example, I tried to please her by playing the piano and adopting her silly values that I was somehow better than most of the friends with whom I hung around—she would remind me that I must never forget that I was a "blue-blood." Where this attitude came from I never knew but it meant to me then that I was different and better.

When I was young, probably around ten, Mother would often question me about my bowel movements. She would want to examine my bowel movements from time to time, and she administered enemas to me every two weeks during times when we were alone in the house. I submitted passively to her attentions and since I was not receiving much loving attention in other ways, her physical touch and attention during the enema episodes aroused me erotically and was something I enjoyed and didn't resist.

In reality, I was caught in an unresolvable dilemma involving two adults pulling me in opposing directions, each vying for my attention in nefarious ways. Regardless of the conflicting pulls, the same emotional messages were communicated: "You are caught in an impasse with no resolution, and you are the ruination of our family because of your behavior!" The early sense I had about this state of affairs was that I had been born into a world where I was booted in the backside for reasons I didn't understand. I was supposed to live without knowing how; therefore, the outcome of this hopeless dilemma was obvious—failure. Feeling fearful, desperate and alone was a generalized emotional state I learned to live with during my childhood years; I did not connect the mood state to any specific thoughts or to any particular interpersonal events—it was just me. It was who I was.

Growing up, I cannot remember anyone ever teaching me how to do anything with the exception of my mother's lessons on table manners and how to be socially polite—for example, holding a door open for a lady and saying 'thank you.' I was a mother's boy who was sullen, angry, and interpersonally submissive. I never learned what a quality relationship was all about—this included relationships with peers, coaches, public school teachers, Sunday school teachers, and adult friends of the family. Thinking back on these times, I trusted no one and was not attached to anyone in a loving relationship. I learned subtle ways to avoid people interpersonally and to avoid the pain of being hurt. I did this by keeping an interpersonal distance, not counting on anyone for help and not expecting anything positive from anyone.

In the fifth grade, I wanted to earn a "knot-hole" ticket to see the city's baseball team play a game. The Shreveport Sports team was managed by Salty Parker. The team would give elementary schools tickets which would then be distributed by the teachers. One day, Ms. Strother handed the tickets out to the class. When she came to my desk, she stopped, looked at me and said, "You don't deserve a ticket." She's also the fifth-grade teacher who made me copy over 150 pages from a large geography book for classroom misbehavior. She assigned me a new set of pages every Friday for most of the school year. I would go home after school and copy the geography book. I've hated geography ever since. Being honest with myself as I look at my early history, I was one of those disruptive children whom all school faculties know, and discuss, and dread having in their classrooms. Since I've become an adult, I've strongly regretted the difficulties I presented to my elementary and junior high school teachers. I know the background talk about such students because I've heard teachers talk many times about how difficult it is to deal with some children. My heart aches for these students as well as for their teachers. In my early years, it was a vicious circle; I had no clue how to escape. Punishment and rejection, not remediation, were the dominant themes I experienced, and learning another way to live would have to wait until much later.

I recall one event when I was twelve years old. It was hot that day in Shreveport, and I was feeling the heat and sweating profusely. While riding my purple Schwinn bike a thought popped into my mind. It came "out of the blue"—I was in the fifth grade and remember it as if it had happened yesterday. The thought went something like this: *"Something is very wrong with me and my life, and I don't know how to fix it."* Today, I know psychodiagnostically, exactly what was going on. Drawing from my clinical knowledge, I would diagnose myself and my mental state as an early-onset case of Persistent Depressive Dysthymic Disorder—an instance of chronic depression with an early adolescent onset. Little did I know at the time that the dysphoria I experienced at twelve years of age and the experiences that exacerbated it would dominate my life to the extent it has.

I've had hearing difficulties since early childhood. I was always told that my hearing problems stemmed from a severe case of diphtheria and high fever at six months that damaged both auditory nerves. In the elementary grades, all I knew was that I couldn't hear as well as my peers. I'm sure it affected my overall school performance in significant ways that I've never fully understood. One instance where my hearing loss did affect my performance happened in the fourth grade. My teacher, Ms. Safford, administered oral spelling tests every Friday on the words we had learned for the week. She would only call out each word two times before moving on. Frequently, I would not be able to decipher the word she called out and since it was only repeated once, I failed most spelling tests. My peers passed these tests, so from an early time, I concluded that I must be "dumb." This self-view of my fourth-grade performance was consistent with my already in-place negative self-perceptions. I lived with this hearing deficit untreated until I was in my late 30s, believing what I had been mistakenly told by specialists that a battery aid would not help. Physicians had told my mother that auditory nerve damage loss could not be improved with an external device. Of course, I believed what she said. Aware now of the behavioral patterns of those with hearing loss, I know that social avoidance and withdrawal is the predominant reaction. My already-in-place social avoidance behavior was simply strengthened by this impairment.

In early adolescence, when it became clear to my parents that I had a hearing deficit, mother took me to Dr. Riggs, an ear-nose-throat doctor. My father never accompanied me to these appointments. I would sit next to her as she drove. She would reiterate what the doctor said after an audiology test and discussion with the physician. Leaving the office I remember feeling inadequate and different over not being able to hear like a normal person. There was also an element of shame involved with my hearing. No encouraging words nor physical touch ever followed these doctor visits, iterated were just the facts of the visit and then, silence during the remainder of the drive.

She also took me shopping to buy clothes. The choices were predominantly hers. I wore the shoes she wanted, and I bought the shirts and pants she selected and felt quietly pleased over my obedience.

Experiences with my mother affected my capability to trust women, to view them as sources of comfort and to relate to them in any way but sexually. I could allow myself to engage in sexual contact without risking any relational dangers involving commitment or personal intimacy. In truth, I had no idea who females were. Looking back, I don't think I ever loved my mother in any authentic way. I needed her and was attached submissively, but I didn't love her. Instead, I was emotionally afraid of her and learned early that if she was displeased with me, she would withdraw her attention. Even though she angered me with her rules and the imposed routines I detested, her rejection was even more frightening. Again, I was never able to balance the threat of her rejection with the soothing comfort of acceptance—the latter was absent. The emotional learning continued throughout childhood. I learned that interpersonal avoidance and detachment were necessary to make survival in my family possible and my negative emotions tolerable.

When I began dating as an adolescent, I brought all this emotional baggage into my attempts at relationship. In junior high school, I liked a girl named Penny whom I visited regularly after school. My mother pushed my father (of course, he acquiesced) to drive by Penny's house to see if we were sitting on the front porch instead of going inside— both her parents worked. I interpreted this event and others like it that I was treading on 'forbidden sexual ground' in dating and doing the wrong thing by leaving my mother. I continued to feel that my sexual feelings were taboo and fraught with danger.

I had a particularly difficult sophomore year in high school when I joined a fraternity known for its antisocial behavior. My choice of peers was clearly skewed in a negative direction. The fraternity initiation was rough and was the only time in my life I remember being tarred (with cup grease) while naked and feathered using chicken feathers and dirt. Then, the initiates were run through a long line and beat with paddles. Afterwards, we were pushed into the back of several pickup trucks and driven naked to the woods and made to jump out. I don't remember how I got home, but my appearance at the door of our squeaky-clean house must have been a startling contrast. My mother, in utter despair as she looked at her grease-monkey fifteen-year-old, said something stunning that I've not forgotten. They were not comforting words. Not remembering exactly what she said, it went something like this: "If you avoid going to the penitentiary, I will be amazed." My social behavior had hit a new low, and again I was aware of digging myself into a hole with no way out. I was an angry, mid-adolescent boy who hated himself for the mess he'd made of things. I just did not know any other way to be.

Many years later as a clinical professor at Virginia Commonwealth University, I was supervising a Ph.D. clinical psychology student in applied clinical practicum. We were discussing developmental sexual issues concerning one of her young adolescent patients. During the supervision hour, I disclosed some of my experiences with my father and mother in regard to early parental sexual education, and she exclaimed, "You got a double whammy: one from your father and one from your mother!" Yes, I did, and the emotional devastation and subsequent effects from these early learning experiences continued to convey the *taboo* nature of sex. These intrapersonal assumptions about sex were never perceptually challenged by seeing two parents holding hands, kissing and caressing each other in my presence—physical sterility predominated. My home, from my perspective, was an emotional desert where the only survival possible was interpersonal avoidance, aloneness and despair.

Mother was also verbally controlling and manipulative with my father, and she dominated my father interpersonally during their marriage. I realized only much later that his incessant teasing of her was very childlike behavior. It was similar to an adolescent boy who didn't know how to relate to a girl, so he teased her, a behavior that precluded any honest dialogue between them.

I spent the last two weeks of my father's life in the intensive care unit sleeping on a cot. The ICU in Shreveport's Schumpert Memorial Hospital allowed such visitation privileges in 1976. During these weeks when he clearly knew he was dying, he refused to talk to my mother— he was dying with a cardiovascular heart disease with comorbid severe hypertension. He died angry with my mother because of her reactions to his increasing physical disability over the last several months of his life (and goodness knows what else). I saw honest anger directed from him toward my mother that I had never observed before. She had verbally chastised him during several social engagements when he nodded off to sleep or was unable to maintain polite social repartee with the guests. Polite sociability was an absolute expectation for her, and his increasing oxygen depletion was not an excusable exception. So, he ended his life angry at his wife and refusing to talk to her. My academic schedule in Virginia required that I leave the ICU in Shreveport and return to work. He died the day after I departed. He was by himself, alone and angry. He went out in the "McCullough Way."

As I've disclosed above, I never liked my mother as a person. I didn't respect her when I was an adolescent, nor did I care for her loud and boisterous demeanor which became more self-centered as she aged. Following my father's death, I was visiting her in Shreveport and we went to a Radio Shack store to buy a stereo component. After a few moments, she rudely berated the clerk for not waiting on her. It was obvious that the clerk was dealing with another customer who had entered before us. Her boorish behavior was an embarrassment.

On another occasion, she asked me one evening what I wanted the next morning for breakfast. I told her I wanted two pieces of toast and coffee. When I came to the breakfast table, she had cooked me scrambled eggs, a large helping of bacon, toast and coffee. I told her again that I didn't want to eat all of this. We became embroiled in an argument over how I must eat a substantial breakfast. She had not paid attention to what I had said the night before. It was another replay of earlier experiences where I felt that I did not exist in her mind—the only thing that counted was what she wanted. I ate two pieces of toast and drank coffee. I did not thank her for breakfast and felt some guilt over my behavior. I had to fight her to maintain any sense of autonomy—a repeated theme throughout my childhood—with iterative emotional reactions of anger and felt-helplessness. When she visited my family in Virginia, I dreaded her coming. She talked incessantly and verbally dominated my family. During her visits, I would leave the room and retire to my office. Nothing I said or did stopped the incessant verbal flow. I don't remember the contents of what she said. It was a constant repetition of facts, memories of earlier events I had heard her describe repeatedly and stories about her church friends in Shreveport. It was the same experience I described earlier when, as a young boy, my parents' friends visited our home—similar to Sartre's book, *Les Mots*. She never conversed to achieve dialogue nor did she appear to listen to what others said—certainly not me. Her talk was more of an exhibitionistic performance. Mother never knew how to talk with others nor to listen seriously to another. Her verbal style was ego-centric, exhibitionistic and one-way.

I had an emotional sense growing up that nothing was mine. Everything I had belonged to others. This was true of the room I slept in, my bed, the furniture in my bedroom, my clothes, my baseball bat and glove and even my first dog, Brownie. The feeling was that my world was 'on loan.' How did I become aware of this sense that nothing was mine? The awareness became obvious much later when my wife and I bought a German shepherd puppy named Münter (German word for 'frisky'). I was in clinical training at the University of Georgia at the time. Münter was the pride of my life and it was then I understood this earlier awareness of not owning anything. Münter belonged to my wife and me. He belonged to no one else, and then I, with some degree of shock, recognized another dimension of my earlier years—I'd never felt that I had a right to possess anything that was all mine. Everything I had was negotiable and belonged to another. I remembered that I had felt the same way with my first dog, Brownie. *Me, mine, my* were all pronouns and adjectives that were foreign words growing up. A sense of autonomy was seriously lacking. Similarly, during high school, my mother was excessively involved in all aspects of my life. In my junior and senior years I began to accumulate academic and social awards. It felt to me that she thrived excessively off my successes. I remember thinking that my successes were really hers, not mine. As stated above, the pattern of a general sense of having little or no possession-aware-ness of what was mine and not mine became much clearer later; at an earlier age, I had had no awareness of this cognitive-emotional deficit.

Summarily, I should note that I was never physically or sexually abused. What I did experience and receive from my father was frequent verbal abuse and punishment; and from my mother, I experienced a cold emo-tional possessiveness that was overwhelming, stultifying and that left me feeling inadequate. The fierceness of my father's late-night verbal tirades reminded me of what a screw-up and failure I was; ironically, he was absent physically and emotionally in all other areas of my life— I was on my own. Our relationship presented emotional barriers to my cognitive-emotional development that were formidable. Left on the field with my mother with no masculine support, I felt inadequate and submissive. I have written extensively about verbal and emotional abuse and neglect in the psychological literature and labeled it *"psychological insults."* These trauma experiences qualitatively differ from the more well-known traumas such as rape, physical beatings, sexual abuse, or parental abandonment; however, when emotional deprivation and ver-bal abuse are encountered on almost a daily basis, they rise to the level of *psychological insults* that become malevolent and maturationally dam-aging in the growing self-perceptions of children. Psychological insults are just as developmentally damaging as the other more well-known categories of maltreatment. Growing up, I incorporated my *father's in-sults* as a self-definition as well as prediction of what my life course would be. *From my mother*, I learned to expect little to nothing in the way of support or felt interpersonal safety from others, particularly from women. The absence of a loving nurturing source of support from my mother combined with her overwhelming emotional invasion into my personal space left me defeated and helpless. Of course, at the time all the above was happening, I was not aware in any abstract sense of what was actually going on. In many ways, I was "living blind" and just trying to survive the *slings and arrows* of daily life—and not doing a very good job. The abstract insights that came later and made much of my early developmental history understandable took years of introspective work and were achieved at a very high personal cost.

My early experiences were chronically abusive and personally costly and have affected me every day of my life. However, they were not permanently disabling because of several facilitative relationships I had later and the fact that I never quit seeking ways to terminate my distress. Much more will be said about this stage of my life in the chapters that follow. This chapter is closed with a description of a novel interpersonal encounter that happened during my last two years of high school and beyond.

Late high school. Several memories in late high school with one adult and peers played a central role in the personal changes I made in the years to come. During the early months of 1953, I met a man who was several years older and a fundamentalist Christian. I'd never heard of a "fundamentalist Christian" before. Scotty Dial began to talk to me about how God loved me. The strange acceptance I experienced during our conversations was novel, and although I was not attracted by his literal interpretations of the Bible, his genuine and authentic demeanor and the fact that he sought me out to talk had a deep effect on me. This experience was a first. These conversations were to have a life-changing effect and motivated me to begin seriously reading the Bible and praying. I was somewhat familiar with the Bible and prayer through my attendance at church, but I'd never understood the relevance in the words I'd heard and read at church as it applied to the desperate state of my life. The encounter with Scotty was qualitatively different than other church relationships I'd had. I discovered a new interpersonal acceptance I'd never experienced before. During the remainder of my junior and senior years in high school, I continued to converse with Scotty and other peers who seemed hungry for the same interpersonal acceptance I found. Without my being really aware of it, my life trajectory started to move toward a path that would lead me far from the road I'd traveled thus far. I entered Louisiana State University in the fall of 1954, and the religious feelings that began in high school ultimately contributed to my enrolling in Perkins School of Theology at Southern Methodist University—a training ground for Methodist Ministers. Why did I enroll at a Methodist seminary? The truth be known, I didn't have anything else better to do after graduation, and I was also curious that perhaps the Methodist ministry might offer a viable professional outlet. For the first time in my life, I embarked on a hunt for a new personal existence that differed from everything I had known up to now. Of course, the old baggage of family trotted right along with me, but I launched out nevertheless. The three years at Perkins Theology School changed my life as I will describe in *Chapter Three* of this book. A few years ago I wrote a poem about these early pre-seminary memories. The poem is an appropriate ending to this section.

Growing up blindfolded
Chained in a personal prison
Trapped like vermin
Confinement was molded.

Didn't know how to break out
To those outside
Learned a stupid social game
That was a dead-end route.

Religion was a part
Of my personal prison,

The God (?) I prayed to
Heard more than I thought.

O'er the eons in the dark
I finally found a door
Toward the world of others
I've learned to walk.

This God (?) heard my sighs
For rescue and help,
Gave me the Courage to Be
Answered my cries.

The sun had risen
Warmed this tired, old traveler
Who exited the space
Of his once dark prison.

Flashback to Chapter One

Reading over the entire text led to an insight concerning a "disconnection" in the flow of my story that occurs between the end of *Chapter One* and the subsequent chapters that follow. *Chapter One* was written about the time when I lived at home in a furnace of abuse and deprivation; the heat of the flames was severe and continuous. The chapters that follow demonstrate a subtle "shift" in experienced abuse severity that, as I reviewed the book later, seemed too abrupt—particularly with no word of explanation why the shift in abuse severity occurred. My felt severity level of abuse decreased once I left home and began my freshman year at Louisiana State University. Thinking back on it now, being out of the house was like withdrawing my hands from a hot stove and experiencing a modicum of relief from the daily abuse and distress. I think the flow of the subsequent chapters reveals this shift in distress level, though the reason for the change was not made explicit. The legacy of my early harsh experiences with both parents left me with a difficult remediation challenge that constitutes the rest of my story in *Chapters Two* through *Seven*. If the reader is aware of this disconnection in stress intensity when beginning *Chapter Two* and thereafter, then I hope I have made it understandable with this comment.

Chapter Two:

Post-Undergraduate College Days

After completing the last chapter and thinking back on my first twenty-one years when I graduated from college, I must honestly admit that I've described a 'failed life.' Why such a harsh verdict? Being honest with myself, at that time I didn't know how to achieve a loving relationship, I didn't trust another person, I was bitter, angry, depressed and felt my future looked empty; and yet, I was at a place in life where I either had to go to work or continue in school. I didn't have any idea who I was nor did I have any plans about a career to pursue. My inner self-destructive feelings and impulses (that I knew so well) were terrifying and these negative thoughts and emotions threatened to break out of my veneer of sociability. In short, I was a very frightened young man going nowhere. Frankly, I'm surprised that I survived psychologically. When I compared myself to many of my fraternity brothers who graduated in the spring, 1958, I knew I was far behind in terms of psychological and social maturity, and now the modicum of safety that university and fraternity life provided was coming to an end. I had to do something. All of us were about twenty-one years old—from a developmental perspective, I was probably operating as an early adolescent. This level of functioning would clearly not facilitate an entrance into the post-university adult world. If one asked why I continued on, seeking, looking, searching for a better way to live while fearing and assuming that I would never discover it, there is only one possible answer I can think of that makes any sense.

Early in my childhood (I have no idea how old I was when I became aware of this), I had a vague sense that I had been born for some reason and there was something I must do with my life. This feeling of having an essential purpose in this existence has always been present, stronger at some times than at others. My undefined sense of purposefulness remained during all the difficulties and screw-ups of childhood: I had been born for a reason, and at twenty-one my heart was a lonely hunter in search of what seemed to be some ill-defined and probably unreachable goal. I wrote a free verse poem years later about this period:

> Faith is living with certainty amidst uncertainty
> It is continuing to build when the plans are lost
> It is being held when there is nothing to hold on to
> It is walking as if on pavement when there is no road
> It is discovering meaning out of despair
> It is searching for something and being found
> Faith is living with certainty amidst uncertainty.

Chapter Three:

The Binkley Boys

So, for no discernible reason other than I didn't know anything else to do, I applied to a United Methodist seminary in Dallas—Perkins School of Theology at Southern Methodist University. I was accepted for the fall semester, 1958, and arrived in Dallas during early September in my green two-door Ford coupe with all my belongings in the back seat. I was assigned a room and roommate in Seligman Hall where all incoming first-year unmarried students were housed. The transition from living in a fraternity house to a seminary dorm-room was jolting—from an animal house to sane housing. The dorm was quieter, it had more of a community feel to it, and all dorm members were actively engaged in pretty much the same didactic activities. All first-year seminarians were required to take a core course curriculum and attend a daily chapel service. Upper-class students delivered the sermons that were critiqued by the seminary faculty. During the first semester, I frequently wondered what I was doing here. Over the next few weeks, I met three fellows who were living in the same dorm and with whom I had much in common—two of them seemed as lost as I was. We began to eat meals together and spent time in lengthy discussions about life issues, our backgrounds, and why we had come to Perkins. One other member admitted that he, like me, had come to seminary because he didn't know anything else to do. Only one of us had made specific plans to enter the Methodist ministry. I didn't know it at the time, but this small group of comrades would evolve into a "band of brothers" that would remain together for almost sixty years. One member, F.D. Dawson, died in April, 2017, and broke the circle which had stood for decades.

F.D. Dawson was my age and was born in Crockett, Texas, a small town in the southeastern part of the state located about 110 miles north of Houston. F.D. was the Golden Gloves Boxing Champion of Beaumont, Texas at age sixteen and, as an adult and in addition to his work duties, remained an ardent hunter, fisherman, camper, and traveler. He graduated from Duke University (as he never let us forget) prior to entering Perkins. He spent his last thirty years with his second wife living in a cabin he had partially built in the woods adjacent to Sam Raburn Lake in Jasper, Texas. F.D. hunted dove and squirrel while at Perkins and went frog-gigging in Turtle Creek, which runs through the center of the Highland Park section of Dallas where SMU is located. Among the four of us, F.D. was probably the most stable and mature: brazenly honest, cocky, assertive, a lady's man and the biggest braggart among us.

The second member was Bobby Williams who was born in San Angelo, in west-central Texas. Bobby was the athlete-basketball player of the group who excelled in basketball at San Angelo Junior College and then played with an athletic scholarship at Southwestern University in Georgetown, Texas. After matriculating from Southwestern, he enrolled at Perkins Seminary. Bob was a generally quiet, soft-spoken individual and one of the most earnest persons I'd ever met. He was also quite idealistic in his belief that all people must be treated equally. He readily admitted he had no idea what this 'God-thing' was nor why he had come to seminary. He was just here.

Our third group member, Jimmy Mayfield, was born in Austin, Texas, and attended San Angelo Junior College with Bobby. Jimmy spent his last two years at the University of Texas and took a back-breaking course load: eighteen hours per semester and working twenty hours a week to underwrite the next semester. Jimmy had little social life nor time to do anything but study and work. He majored in english and co-majored in history, philosophy and education. During his senior year at UT, he fell into a serious major depressive episode and became very suicidal. He told us on several occasions that he had planned how he would take his life. Jimmy was the "free-verse poet" and was known among our first-years at Perkins as the "community cynic." His cynicism was excessive and his forté was quoting Friedrich Nietzsche. In a moment of extreme and surprising honesty, he confided to us that he had come to Perkins Seminary for only one reason—to try to find HOPE to keep on living. With this accidental collision of four individuals who had ended up in Seligman Hall in September, 1958, with very little idea why we were here, I found my niche among three seminary misfits; however, the existential stakes were high for all of us, each in our own idiosyncratic way.

As the fall semester progressed, we decided to move off campus and move into an apartment. First year students at Perkins were expected to live on campus, so we quickly ran afoul of the standard housing policy at the seminary. We persisted against the strong wishes of our mentors, and at the end of the semester in late December, we set up housing several blocks off campus in a small duplex on Binkley Avenue.

Personally, I knew that by becoming involved in this group, I was moving into a risky interpersonal domain because my first experience at living with others (viz. my family) had been a disastrous involvement while my second (with fraternity brothers) had enabled me to maintain a convenient sphere of escape from developmental growth and maturity. Somehow, this move portended to be a different kind of endeavor and it was—I was scared.

Evening Discussions. Living with three comrades, who quickly became known in the seminary as the "Binkley Boys," offered several experiences that were novel. One involved participating in extended evening conversations about a variety of topics. During my undergraduate days, fraternity brothers did not register for the same classes; hence, they were not in my courses. In four years, I cannot remember one class where a fraternity brother was in the same course. Such was not the case in seminary. We all took the same courses for the first two years. Our similar curriculum afforded many opportunities for discussion that were not available at LSU. One evening we discussed a theological topic involving an existential New Testament theologian named Rudolph Bultmann. His radical views involved rethinking the New Testament by omitting its mythological language—*demythologizing the text* Bultmann called it. He argued that such language as the virgin birth, angels, voices from heaven, stilling a storm on the Sea of Galilee with a word-command, etc., fit nicely in the context of the pre-scientific ancient world; but to scientific twentieth-century individuals, such language was foreign, was not understood and frequently led to a rejection of the entire New Testament.

One member of our group, F.D., argued strongly for an extreme Bultmannian approach to New Testament interpretation while the rest of us opined that a rejection of all mythological language was an excessive alternative. None of us viewed the myths as being literally true, but we felt that extirpating all mythological language would severely compromise the meaning of the text. The debate continued for several hours with no one shifting his perspective.

Growing up in an authoritarian family where there were no open discussions about anything because parental views were ultimate was vastly different from the Binkley group. Disagreement, at least from me, on issues that were 'unquestionable' in my family was not listened to nor tolerated. Among these colleagues, I was in a different interpersonal environment: agreement was not our goal; negative judgment or comments on the adequacy or quality of one's view were not tolerated; sitting, listening and reacting were acceptable behaviors; tolerating divergence of opinion was important; and trying to understand the others' beliefs was of utmost value. I, unknown to the others, brought an entire lifetime understanding of conversation to these evening discussions that made me uncomfortable. My father's inability or refusal to listen to any opinion I might have comingled with his frequent comments of "Ne'r mind" that shut down all discussion on my part and my mother's emotional and behavioral withdrawal in the face of disagreement constituted the only conversational landscape I knew. Here in the Binkley House, I was thrust into a foreign land, conversation-wise, and at the outset, I felt awkwardly out of place. With no experience, I was expected to be a verbal participant and contribute. During these early discussions, I said little and was hesitant to express opinions. In fact, I wasn't even sure what my opinions were. Thinking for myself or taking myself seriously enough *to have* an opinion presented a distinctly novel challenge. But one thing was clear: interpersonal avoidance was not going to work here. I knew that sooner or later I was going to have to get in the game. At first, I didn't know how.

Talking to someone *with* the goal of understanding the other was new—feeling interpersonally safe in a group is the first requisite for honest verbal behavior. Frankly, not having felt interpersonally safe around peer groups in the past had resulted in a longstanding habit of inhibiting my thoughts and remaining fearful to voice opinions. Learning to experience interpersonal safety around my comrades in the Binkley

House was not quickly acquired. At first, there were too many compet-
ing and distracting thoughts. *If I say this, what will others think? What if
I'm wrong? What might I be overlooking? Do I have my facts right? etc.* I
also learned something else: if certain emotive experiences like feelings
of interpersonal safety are not present in my learning repertoire, I could
not verbalize opinions without a concerted internal effort. I'd never before had any reason to challenge this inhibiting fear. There was something about these nightly interactions that attracted me. I wanted to be
a part, and I very much wanted to learn how to participate. I began to
deliberately risk expressing myself. Favorable reactions from the others
resulted. This was different from my past experiences. I continued taking risks and was never shouted down or made to feel inferior. Rather,
my comrades seemed to appreciate my views, and in some instances,
what I said modified the way one or more of them looked at some issue.
I began to feel empowered by these nightly interactions and my verbal
reactions became more frequent. I was becoming a participant!

Something qualitatively different was happening inside me, and over
time, these newly learned behaviors challenged everything I had previously learned about myself and my relationship with others. The trajectory of interpersonal avoidance which had characterized my life up
to now began to slowly turn around. My emotional experience was
changing as fear was being replaced with confidence, and I was beginning to take my views more seriously than ever before. I experienced
the reactions of others as positive, and the prominence of the old felt
rejection was being undercut by a sense of interpersonal acceptance.
Lastly, my conversational behavior was shifting toward a growing ability
to listen seriously to others. Words, I was learning, were tools to make
feelings understood and not simply tools to be used to relate facts. This
was a far cry from my earlier learning when, as a little boy, I sat in my
house on the second floor steps and listened to my parents' guests use
thousands of words that only expressed emotionless facts—*Les Mots*

(words without meaning for Sartre). For me, words were becoming *les mots avec du sens* (words *with* meaning).

As the spring semester moved toward the early days of May, the subject of our discussions left the purely didactic and took on a different note. We talked about earlier experiences with parents, siblings and friends. I discovered I was not the only one who had felt rejection from parents and who had recoiled in despair from fears of abandonment. One individual disclosed that he never liked or respected his mother. Another confided that he and his father had never been close nor had they engaged in serious conversation. A third divulged that his views of God had been called into serious question in college, and the threat of losing a long-standing existential worldview had left him feeling empty, alone and concluding that his life was no longer worth living. I began to reveal some of my earlier experiences and express the emotional wasteland I'd brought to the group. No one tried to repair or fix anything the other said. We listened and accepted what was said. Again, such responses were new and comforting. I was not alone in my history of despair. Others had experienced the same feelings and felt as I did. At this point, we didn't have suggestions that might offer alternatives to the idiosyncratic dilemmas we disclosed to one another. At this point, just being heard and not judged was sufficient for me. The extraordinary truth of these encounters was that we would awaken the next morning after our disclosures the previous evening and would still be accepted as before—something more was increasingly binding us together than just our words. I was discovering an emotional caring that I had not experienced before.

One evening, one in the group revealed how close he had come to taking his life during the month prior to our first semester at seminary. This topic received an unusual reaction. The reaction was more than just benign acceptance. Each group member disclosed how personally devastating such an act would have been and how what we had now would have been precluded. It became clear that the individual disclosing suicide, if such a step were to be taken, would inflict severe personal damage on each one of us and, as noted, would also destroy our group. In short, the consequences would be significantly felt by each member and have severe repercussions. The message was obvious: what we do in this group affects everyone and there is no longer neutrality of group membership among the Binkley Boys. I had never felt such attachment being a member of my own family; for me, at least, it had been more of an 'every person for himself' sort of an existence. I never thought much about how my behavior affected others. It was just me, me, me. The Binkley group environment propelled me into another mode where I was learning to think of others and how what I did affected others. For the first time, I was learning that there was a big world beyond the personal space that was ME!

In our own way, each of us was on a hunt. We were looking for meaning in our lives while simultaneously reading and studying some of the most outstanding theologians of the mid-twentieth century. Paul Tillich's view of Divine Acceptance or "being grasped by the Ground of Being" comes to mind. We spent hours discussing what this could possibly mean. None of us had had such an experience with transcendence, but in a more mundane way, all of us had experienced the strong mutual acceptance within the group. This led to more discussion about how our daily encounters with one another were mirroring in some ways the great theological constructs we read about. Dietrich Bonhoeffer's view of "being a Christ (brother) to one another" provided another avenue for discussion. One of our group articulated Bonhoeffer's axiom one night at dinner: "As crazy as it sounds, we are becoming brothers to one another." I'd never had a brother before. In fact, only one of us had. F.D had two younger brothers while Jimmy and Bobby didn't. I'm not sure when this statement was made, but it revealed that the process of attachment between the four of us was deepening and becoming meaningful. The existential meaning all of us searched for was literally being actualized among us. We were not "talking about" being brothers; becoming brothers was actually happening in the present. I was stunned by the 'brother' comment, and it is still meaningful to me almost sixty years later. "We are becoming brothers" was, indeed, a novel experience and beckoned me to a different life path.

Once again, the stark contrast between my earlier years and what I was experiencing among the Binkley Boys was startling. I learned several things about brothers. Brothers love one another. Brothers have one another's back. Brothers support one another during troubled times. Brothers are honest, and while there was always a considerable amount of baloney going on in interactions, the seriousness of the bond trumped the frivolous. Brothers share their lives. Brothers trust one another over time when their relationship continues through crises and trials. Everything I was discovering in this group challenged the malicious and dangerous worldviews I had brought to seminary, made me challenge my strongly-held negative self-view, and offered an alternative salubrious view: *I was a worthy human being.* These interpersonal outcomes were totally unexpected when I first moved in with these guys and could not have happened without the close living environment afforded in the Binkley House. Slowly, my life's trajectory of personal failure started to turn around, but the process was very slow and not smooth.

Before leaving this section, one memory of an intense evening discussion comes to mind. During our first year, late in the spring semester, we all attended a lecture of Paul Tillich, a Lutheran theologian, and heard a presentation of his doctrine of salvation. Tillich relied heavily on the Latin root word *salvus* to explain his theological viewpoint. Salvus literally means 'healthy' or 'whole' and he applied it to every act of healing—the healing of physical and psychological disease, demon possession, enslavement to sin, and ultimately, to the overwhelming destruction of death. Salvation takes place in a temporal or historical context, that is, in the here and now. This particular evening, our group gathered in the living room and discussed the lecture. Bobby began to talk of healing moments, *salvus moments*, he had experienced in our group. He confided he felt a belongingness that he had never experienced before and confessed that being one of the Binkley Boys had altered his negative opinion of himself and of others. He then said the words that had not been spoken before: "I feel like you all have loved me, and I've never felt this way before." Jimmy admitted he had discovered a reason to live through participating in our group and that the relationships had been the medium through which this newly found healing or *salvus* had been imparted. F.D. said, frankly, that he loved each one of us and described how this group was the most important thing that had ever happened to him. There was not much left for me to say. All that had been disclosed expressed what I too had discovered but I did add that while I had never had a brother, I had three sitting with me now and the experience was one of felt safety and strong support. I also remember saying that I was feeling a tremendous emotion of gratitude for the healing that had been taking place in my life since we started living together. I did not have the courage to say that I loved each one of them at that time, but I did. *Salvus* had been actualized among the Binkley Boys over the past several months, and Tillich's words aptly described what was happening: *healing within the lives of four young men.*

Earlier learning experiences in my family had left indelible marks on me and were not hastily revised. It took years to achieve a thorough turn-around as regards destructive behaviors, thoughts and emotions. The new experiences I had on Binkley Avenue were showing me what my life could be while concomitantly laying down new neural connections (via novel experiences) that had not been present before. In short, and I say this again, new patterns of behavior were being shaped in me THAT HAD NOT BEEN IN MY BRAIN BEFORE! Change came slowly because I was living out a qualitatively different and difficult pattern of behavior with others and practicing it daily; I was actually living it out and not thinking about or talking about being different. These lessons learned from actual living were to have an immense influence on my entire clinical career, not to mention my personal life.

Over the years, I've often asked myself how I was able to tolerate the unfamiliar interpersonal territory that living with the Binkley Boys represented—it would have been easy to leave. Their acceptance and support was the *key element* that provided the staying power. Interpersonal acceptance was the *glue* that bound me to the group. I'd never have been able to stay the course nor tolerate the newness of relationship had I not experienced the positive and powerful attachments of relationship. Tillich was right; being grasped by the interpersonal acceptance of comrades was the source of courage that enabled me to stay with the group. I should also note that I was not becoming more religious as the days in seminary wore on, but I was certainly recognizing the relevance of our theological study with what was happening to me and my brothers during this intense period of personal growth and struggle.

Household Duties. To maintain a house and prevent it from becoming a landfill or junk-pile, particularly among a group of young adult males, quickly required that a distribution list be made of upkeep responsibilities. This event was an occasion of another startling personal revelation. I realized that I had been so egocentrically focused on "surviving the hell of my family" that I had never learned how to be a responsible member of my family. All I had had to do in college was put my trash in a wastebasket and housekeeping would remove it. Earlier, my mother had done all the room cleaning for me. Household maintenance became a source of conflict for our group during the spring semester. As it turned out, none of us had previously been required to discharge assigned duties to keep a living space viable. Household chores were assigned by group decision: vacuuming the house and dusting, cleaning the bathroom (we had two bathrooms), cooking meals, buying food, washing dishes, paying the utility bills and monthly rent, keeping clothes picked up and not throwing one's dirty clothes on the living room furniture or on other chairs throughout the house, putting away one's washed clothes and not throwing them on the bedroom floor where others had to walk, and emptying the trash in the house and putting it in large trash bins in the alley for county pick-up. Not surprisingly, we discovered that some were better cooks than others, some cleaned more thoroughly than others, some were better bookkeepers, and so on. A list of weekly duties was posted on the kitchen bulletin board.

I was assigned to trash pick-up duty on a daily basis and required to vacuum the rugs and dust the interior once per week. Check-offs on the list of duties were done after an assigned chore had been performed. During the weeks after the chores had been assigned, I forgot to pick up the trash and take our considerable daily mess to the alley bin. I was called out for my negligence. The feedback came in a different form than earlier familial feedback where I had been chastised and labeled a "screw-up." This feedback was more of a brotherly, "Get off your ass, McCullough, and take the trash out!" Everyone got feedback at the supper table or in evening discussions. So, the critique was spread around to everyone until we shaped up and began to function together as a 'coordinated household team.' After I failed miserably at the cooking duty, I was not assigned to cook again. Washing the dishes I could do and bookkeeping came easily, but I never mastered the culinary art.

What I learned was again a novel experience. To be a member of a group required that I do certain things for the good of the collective. This lesson was not easy to come by. Frankly, I'd never thought of anyone but myself, but now I was behaving in ways that put others before me. The group's well-being, as trivial as it might sound, involved cleaning the house, washing dishes, keeping the books and paying bills. If I slacked off, the group was affected in a palpable way. A further realization was that I was a necessary cog in the daily functioning of the Binkley Boys' House and was counted on to carry my share of the load. Again, no one had ever counted on me for anything; consequently, I'd never felt a part of anything.

Trying to survive during my earlier developmental history forced me psychologically to turn inward and precluded my learning how to relate successfully to the world of others; it also resulted in a more horrific consequence: my personal struggles left me interpersonally avoidant and disconnected perceptually from my social environment. My generalized worldview was that what I did really didn't matter in any essential way. This was probably the most pernicious outcome from my abusive upbringing. I was alone and adrift aimlessly until I failed to complete my assignments and take out the trash and clean the house. Then, my first wake-up call came on Binkley Avenue. I was reminded that my behavior *did* have consequences and that I had better get off my ass and get moving. Such moments and many that followed always came as revelations to me.

Sometimes when we stand at an existential junction in the road and see where we've been and where we must go, the perspective in the moment seems overwhelming and frightening. I faced such existential intersections many times living with the brothers. I would gasp in horror at the social and emotional desert I'd previously lived in and would think to myself: *"Jim, you were never humanized or taught to live in a world with other people. How did you ever survive and make it this far?"* These intersection moments have left me NEVER taking for granted the salubrious histories many of my friends and colleagues had and that they can describe so casually. I hear others speak of having wonderful childhood memories, having loving and thoughtful parents, recalling wonderful family memories, and sharing intimate times with their loved ones. All I can do at such times is sit quietly and think to myself: *"You are so fortunate and you don't even know it. You take for granted what I never knew, and it would be difficult for you to even comprehend the world I came from."* I usually say nothing at such times and remain a bit sad.

The Binkley Boys and Apartheid in Dallas. Many of our seminary classes were held in the morning, and after the ten o'clock class, we would walk across Hillcrest Avenue to get coffee at a large corner drugstore (not called a pharmacy in those days) on the corner of McFarland Street and Hillcrest Avenue. A long row of swivel stools lined the lunch counter on the left wall where patrons sat and ordered shakes, hamburgers, fries and coffee. There were probably twelve or fifteen stools at the counter. One of our student colleagues was an African American named Nat Lacy. Dr. Lacy later became the first African American to join the Perkins Seminary faculty. Nat and the Binkley Boys would often talk after class, and he visited the Binkley House a number of times. When it was time for a coffee break, Nat couldn't join us because blacks were not served at the drugstore counter. About this time, Martin Luther King began his sit-ins and demonstrations in other southern cities. The four of us decided that from now on, if Nat was willing, he would be invited to join us for coffee. On the first morning Nat went with us, we agreed to dress in suits with ties and coats. As it turned out, the coats came in handy. All four of us along with a number of other seminary students entered the drugstore filling up all the stools; then, we asked the waitress for coffee. She was somewhat nonplussed and called the manager. When he spotted Nat, he said loudly that "niggers are not allowed to be served at this counter." We continued to sit and politely asked for coffee. He asked us to leave and when we didn't move, he said something like this: "Alright you sons-of-bitches, I'll show you how we

52

treat niggers who act like white folk." He left the front of the store and returned shortly with a large pesticide spray machine; turning it on, he sprayed the entire counter-section of the store with *dichlorodiphenyl-trichloroethane,* which is a fancy name for the more well-known pesticide, DDT. Soon, the spray had spread throughout the store. For those who might not be aware of this pesticide, it was banned for use in the United States during the 1960s by the newly formed Environmental Protection Agency. The manager sprayed us for almost two hours, as we continued to sit with coats pulled up tightly over our heads. He continued to shout obscenities at us. The spraying stopped when police entered and escorted us out of the drugstore. He was still yelling when we left the store. This was the first civil rights demonstration conducted in Dallas and the *Dallas Morning News,* the city's large morning daily, never mentioned the event. This was also the first time that I saw, first-hand, what was driving apartheid in the south—violent hatred of blacks to a degree that I didn't know existed. This was civilized Dallas and the business stood directly across from the upper middle-class Southern Methodist University. The Binkley Boys participated in further demonstrations in Dallas, but we never again encountered a reaction like the drugstore debacle. This was also the first time our quartet had stood together in such a collective mess. We knew we might be headed into a firestorm, but our friendship with Nat eclipsed the fears. I had an unusual reaction to the sit-in. I had crossed a barrier that was a southern societal taboo. I had done it with a band of brothers who stood with me. I was left with a feeling of pride and an emotion of belongingness. Once again, I was plowing new ground with comrades who felt as I did about the injustice of southern apartheid. I would have never done something like this by myself—but, with brothers, it was doable.

I never knew how my father found out about my Dallas sit-in participations, but they enraged him and he threw everything in his negative verbal repertoire at me—and to think that I did this for nothing less than for 'niggers.' He was terrified that his way of life was being threatened by a son who, he opined, was out of control. I understood this, but I psychologically walked away knowing that I could not go back to Shreveport and walk back into my old life. Shortly thereafter, my mother let me know her views, in a harsh tone that was a bit unusual, when she remarked: "Perkins has ruined you and turned you into someone I don't know." So, in the tradition of Thomas Wolfe, I clearly knew that I could NOT go home again. The return-bridge to my earlier beginnings was burned and broken. It was straight ahead into an unknown future. In being brutally honest, while this was true physically and geographically, it was certainly not totally true psychologically. I still had a long way to go to fully rectify a 'failed life.'

The Binkley Group after SMU. Two of our group continued to demonstrate in civil rights activities after we graduated from Perkins in June, 1961. F.D. went to Washington in 1963 when M.L. King delivered his "I Have a Dream" speech. In 1965, he also marched over the Selma Bridge with King only to get hit with water cannons, beaten by police batons and attacked by German shepherd dogs. Bobby traveled to Mississippi, and in Philadelphia, participated with the 'freedom riders' demonstrations. Some of the riders were severely injured and lost their lives; I always felt that Bobby was very fortunate to emerge from Mississippi alive and unscathed. I didn't have the requisite courage to accompany either of them.

F.D. came to visit my wife and me in Richmond, Virginia, to attend the August, 2013, fiftieth anniversary March on Washington. Having heard King many years before, he passionately wanted to celebrate the event again. I took him to the Amtrak train station in Richmond at 6:00 A.M. He arrived in Washington and was on the Washington Mall by 8 A.M. Surprisingly, he was back in Richmond by 2:30 P.M. and came back depressed, as sad as I'd ever seen him. F.D. said there had been no music, no "We Shall Overcome," only a few political notables present, and hundreds of speakers lined up for brief, two-minute speeches. At the end of each two-minute speech, a very loud and insulting speaker blared out "TA DA, TA DA, TA DA..." This onerous noise continued until the individual exited the microphone. Most of the speeches were hostile diatribes against social and racial inequities and repetitive calls for a more just racial, social and economic society. What also upset F.D. was the total absence of any *unifying theme* for the march. He found this thematic vacuum standing in stark contrast to the former march fifty years earlier; instead, hundreds of thousands of noisy people wandered around yelling slogans, carrying placards or were congregated in small groups wearing different colored T-shirts with different social agendas written on them. A fragmentation of separate agendas, not unity, characterized the chaos of this March on Washington. In returning to our home and in subsequent discussions during the remainder of his visit, F.D. said, over five years ago, that the March symbolized to him that our great land was hopelessly mired in, seriously fractured with, and divided by a collision of multiple agendas. To him, our national future did not look promising after the chaos of the March on Washington. Ironically, I had naively thought that the civil rights movement we participated in almost fifty-five years earlier and that had led to many legislative breakthroughs would solve many of our national problems. It didn't.

My encounters with apartheid in Dallas became again another existential junction or turning point enabling me to compare and contrast my limited pre-seminary worldview with the huge unknown world of people that lay beyond Shreveport. I knew that I could never return to the old ways of the South with its primitive-tribal values and authoritarian principles—my home had been a microcosm of such views. While I would not characterize myself as free from the old, I had tasted personal independence and the sweet smell of the open road to personal freedom.

Now, I faced another challenge which was new. I was leaving the Binkley Group as we, upon graduation, were scattering to the four winds. Texas, being the big state that it is, is divided into five Methodist Church conferences. Each conference was presided over by a bishop. F.D. was going to the Texas Conference and would be a fifth-generation Dawson preacher in that conference. His great-great grandfather Dawson had been a Methodist circuit-rider. Jimmy and Bobby were assigned to church parishes in the Southwest Texas Conference, and I was going to the Louisiana Conference to start a new church parish in Baton Rouge. We were 'locked and loaded' with a mid-twentieth century Protestant existential view of a God whom we believed was working towards a "new world order;" and we were being assigned to church parishes embedded in the "old world order." It was to be a brutal reckoning for three of us. One was ejected from his Conference following his divorce—a move not allowed by Methodist ministers at the time. He was later reinstated. Another ended up in Texas politics after a serious and ugly segregation confrontation with his bishop who would not support African Americans being invited to join him in his worship services. He subsequently left the Methodist ministry and became the chief of staff of a Texas governor. He remained active in Texas politics for years, even serving as mayor of a city in Texas. I knew soon after completing seminary and after three years in the parish that being a Methodist minister was not my "cup of tea." In 1964, I resigned my ordination, married, and then entered clinical psychology training at the University of Georgia. From our original Binkley Boys' seminary group, two of us remained and retired in the ministry and two left the profession.

As an aside, and I was not thinking about this when I resigned my ordination in 1964, even though the Methodist ministry was not my calling, I have never lost the sense that I was born to fulfill a purpose. As a young boy, I had felt the strong pull of the "Golden Cord" and the sense of it remained through my early years and is still with me today. That life purpose was to be actualized and fulfilled in my forty-seven-year career as a clinical psychologist.

The 60-year History of the Binkley Boys (1958-2018). F.D. died of bladder cancer at 3:33 A.M. on Monday, April 17, 2017. How do I know the time? I woke up and looked at the clock at 2:58 A.M. Monday morning. I remember the thought crossing my mind: *F.D. is in trouble.* Then I fell off to sleep and was awakened again by his voice. It was not audible, but I heard it in my mind. He said, "Goodbye, Jim." Rising up and quickly looking at the clock next to the bed, I read, 3:33 A.M. The next morning his wife, Alice, called and said that he had died. She'd gone to check on him about 3:00 A.M. and found him sleeping. He had died sometime after 3:00 A.M. because when she looked in again at 4:00 A.M., he was gone. I told Alice that I knew when he died. "It was 3:33 A.M." Then, I told her what had happened between the two of us. There are three Binkley Boys left.

I wrote a poem for F.D.'s funeral in Jasper, Texas on May, 6, 2017.

Taught, instructed and commanded to love the other
Since we were old enough to walk,
We heard these words in church and home
Before we could even talk.

No one ever taught us love's cost
What to do when we loved and the one we loved, lost.
What to do when we loved and lost our nerve -
When we lost Ferd.

Oh, I know we can celebrate his life, but the question remains
What do I do after blowing my horn, saying my words and singing anthems of praise?
What do I do with the emptiness, the void, recollections that burn with memories raised?

What do I do when I can't reach out with words and hear his coming back?
What do I do when I can't hit his shoulder and feel flesh on skin?
What do I do with the nothingness that haunts my soul when losing my kin?

Like Ezekiel, I hear the words: "Mortal, who are you to question My Ways?"
I question, we question!
I have to ask about love's cost
I must know why life is a coffer full of loss,
The agony, the pain in my quiet moments of being alone
Are not stilled by sighs or deepest moans.

I hurt because the brother I loved is gone,
The only comfort are the words from the morn -
The first Day of the New Creation,
When an angel told the Marys, "The Teacher is raised,
And you must not be afraid."

For someone who had run from relationships all his earlier life, I have, in later life, been fortunate to have had wonderful, meaningful and sustaining friendships. For me, the intersection in the road that marked the beginnings of my life turn-around and the beginnings of repairing a "failed life" was the Binkley Group in which I encountered three guys who became lifelong comrades and brothers. F.D. and I roomed together for several years, and I learned to love him and all that made up this puckish and talented guy. He was a "man's man" who never backed away from any challenge that I knew about. He taught me some things about boxing, and I'm glad I never had to go several rounds with him. He was able to play the cards well that life dealt him. When the bishop ejected him from the Methodist ministry because of an "unacceptable" divorce, he returned to the church sometime later and was chastised for his 'unacceptable behavior' by being appointed to several churches that were in desperate straits. F.D. turned every one of these parishes into thriving, vibrant communities. He retired after serving an appointment to a large parish where, once again, he succeeded. I feel fortunate that I was able to walk with this brother as long as I did.

Jimmy and Bobby are both retired and living in Austin. Of the four of us, Jimmy was the most successful churchman, a poet of note and a writer of church hymns. After graduation from seminary, he was fortunate to work with senior parish ministers who taught him the ropes of running churches and helped him advance through the church's hierarchy. Jimmy avoided the interpersonal career hardships that Bobby and I had and that put us in a bad light with our bishops. He was always the tactful one who could say what was needed and keep his cool in the process while the rest of us lost ours. This disciplined skill served him well and helped him bring *salvus* (healing) to many of his parishioners during a long and distinguished career.

Bobby was and is a brother who always, like me, had trouble keeping his mouth shut. Extremely idealistic about the intrinsic worth of the poor and outcast, particularly among the African and Mexican Americans in south Texas, Bobby was always in the middle of some organizational (church or political) skirmish. He never understood why so many parishioners in the Methodist Church as well as the citizens in Texas politics were not interested in helping needy populations. His heart is as wide as the "Big Sky" in Texas and personal generosity was always his greatest asset. Bobby taught me about generosity and why it was so important in interpersonal relationships. He always had my back, and I would trust him with my life. This is still true today. When I had some of my worst moments in seminary, Bobby was the one I would talk with; he always had the gift and patience to strengthen me emotionally and help me get back in the game.

In summary, I do not think of the Binkley Boys as "Christians" in a traditional, pietistic way. Rather, they are and were what I would label as a non-religious cohort, authentic and honest. This crusty, obscene-talking bunch of guys created a loving brotherhood. Through these loving relationships over a lifetime, I started and am still learning how to love and maintain interpersonal relationships.

My First Job in the Parish. I was appointed to start a new church parish in North Baton Rouge, Louisiana. This section of Baton Rouge was populated by blue-collar workers who worked at the railroads, Allied Chemical, ESSO (EXXON today), and other refineries and chemical companies. The ninety-mile stretch south from Baton Rouge to New Orleans became known as the "chemical alley" because of numerous refineries and chemical plants along Louisiana State Highway 61. My parishioners, many of whom worked on shifts, religiously carried their metal lunch boxes and thermos bottles to work. They loved beer and drank black Luzianne coffee that was so strong it made my hair stand on end. I was one of the "educated guys" who clearly was not a blue-collar worker. But, I liked the informality of the area and spent most of my time sitting in kitchens drinking café au lait with the parishioners.

I fit in well with the members and fished often with them in the bayous hunting for largemouth bass which were plentiful. Being single at the time, my first apartment cost fifty dollars a month and since my starting salary was only three hundred dollars, rent, phone bills, food, clothes and gasoline meant that I had little left over to spend on other things.

I enjoyed working with the people in the parish but realized during the first year that being a minister was not how I wanted to spend the rest of my career. I was constantly called "preacher," a moniker I never liked. The parishioners kept reminding me that having me around meant they had to clean up their language—it took a while for them to realize that this was not necessary.

The name of our church parish was *St. Luke's Methodist Church*. I selected the name because St. Luke was alleged to have been a physician and healer. I liked the thought of creating a place where *salvus* predominated. I performed one wedding while I was there. The wedding was held in the home of a parishioner as we didn't yet have a building. The father of the bride was a burly man who weighed over three hundred pounds and his wife was not much smaller. The bride and groom were all decked out in their fancy clothes. I launched into the service. Shortly after the ceremony began, the family dog, a small ChowChow, starting snapping and biting my ankle, gently at first and then harder. He would grab my sock and pull—balancing and standing upright became increasingly difficult. At times, his bite hurt, and I finally glanced over to the bride's father, the fat man, hoping to get some assistance. He had an amused smirk on his face at my obvious difficulties. No one made a move to help nor did anyone seem to care what the dog was doing to my ankle. Finally, I said to the couple that either the dog had to go or I was leaving. The bride, in her flowing white gown scooped the dog up; I'm not sure what happened next but I guess she locked the dog in a back room. The crisis ended and I thought to myself:

"What have I gotten myself into!" I completed the ceremony, the groom kissed the bride and everyone looked happy. I left and put merthiolate on my ankle.

Looking back, I was successful in the parish of St. Luke's as we built a nice building during my third year. We also took in a number of new members. The only problem I had was that the congregation was delinquent paying my monthly salary—$350 a month. I received a $50 raise the second year. At one point, the church was three months in arrears, and my phone was about to be disconnected, I was almost evicted from my apartment and my Volkswagen was about to be repossessed. I went to the pulpit one Sunday morning and said a very brief sermon. The gist was that financially, I was in serious trouble because of a lack of salary and though I enjoyed working with the congregation, I was not coming back to St. Luke's until they paid my salary. My salary was paid the next day.

Chapter Four:

Henry R. Olivier, M.D.

During my first year in the parish, I joined a group of Baton Rouge ministers, psychiatrists, other medical specialists and social workers who met monthly discussing mental health readings. A psychiatrist in Baton Rouge was a member of the group and was an avid participant. His comments during the meetings always interested me. I had remained depressed after leaving seminary, and I decided to address some unfinished personal issues. After one meeting ended, I spoke to the psychiatrist, Dr. Olivier, who was also a trained psychoanalyst, and asked if I could make an appointment. He said 'yes,' and I did. I saw Hank (as I began to call him) several times a week for over two years.

From the outset, he was a comfortable individual to be around because he was himself and never played the frequently encountered professional role that held patients at arms' length. We began treatment with me lying on a bluish-green vinyl couch raised on one end. Hank sat in the rear and smoked Salem menthol cigarettes - no one worried about "second-hand smoke" in the 1960s. At first, there were long periods of silence as I had no idea what to say. Hank waited patiently. At some point, I began to describe my life-story and we were off and running on a constructive treatment trajectory that I'm still drawing strength from. At eighty-two years of age, I see things differently than I did at age twenty-four. In remembering some of the events I disclosed with Hank, I am looking back through the lens of many years. The myriad memories I discussed certainly described me as I was then, not now.

After my seminary experiences with the Binkley Brothers, I was prepared for the quasi-psychoanalysis with Hank. I use the word, quasi-psychoanalysis, because Hank, although adopting many of the assumptions and treatment methods of Sigmund Freud, deviated significantly compared to Freud's praxis of psychotherapy, particularly in regard to the way he related interpersonally with patients. Freud required strict adherence to a therapist neutrality role prohibiting clinicians from becoming personally involved with patients. Expressing the clinician's personal opinions, values or attitudes was strictly verboten. Freud also described the relationship psychotherapists establish with patients as a "counter-transference" domain, writing that it was taboo for practitioners to 'step over the line' and use themselves as a source of influence or change. Change was all up to the patient and the only allowable therapist's reactions were rare cognitive-emotive-behavioral interpretations. Thus, the optimal counter-transference role must be one of strict neutrality so as not to influence or interfere in the free-associations of the patient.

Notably, Dr. Olivier did not adhere to Freud's role proscription, so, from the outset, I encountered someone interpersonally who didn't maintain a neutrality role nor did he withhold verbal reactions to me concerning what I said, did and thought. Freud would have been appalled—Hank could have cared less. Shortly after treatment began, he started calling me "Jimbo."

I covered all the remembered "hot spots" (hurtful memories) of my early childhood and adolescence. There were periods with Hank where I anticipated rejection. It never came. This was difficult at first because of its novelty. I was sitting in the presence of an accepting, older authority figure that didn't react to me as my father had. An accepting interpersonal reality personage was foreign, unfamiliar and unnerving in the beginning of our relationship. I also discussed situations where I had performed well and received another different reaction: "I thought you told me you were a nothing, a failure. And now, you tell me about something good you did. Have you been lying to me!! You did great here!" I would be somewhat shocked and remain silent; here, in the midst of situational events which I had previously judged to be only fair, I was now being responded to in an unconditional, positive manner. One such example involved my fifth grade teacher who, as I related earlier, for a disciplinary infraction made me copy the large geography book. Once, when I turned in my weekly copy-assignment, Ms. Strother opened her desk drawer, and I saw a set of my handwritten papers she had earlier accused me of not turning in. I exclaimed loudly, "These are my papers in your drawer that you said I had not written! What are you doing here?" She quickly closed the drawer and the exchange ended with no answer. She never answered my question. I had mentioned this to my parents and they had just shrugged. I returned to my seat and for many months, I continued copying. Hank said the teacher was wrong and unfair and that I had done the right thing to assert myself. Many childhood events I described seem quite trivial as I write about them now, but taken together as a history that constituted a damning legacy of rejection, they denoted an earlier part of my life filled with self-rejection, failure and unworthiness. Hank's consistent acceptance while I was talking about failures, in fear and trembling, gradually modified the negative self-reactions. Something in me was changing. I was becoming less frightened to discuss failures and more confident that what awaited me was his interpersonal acceptance. Feeling interpersonally safe and less vulnerable increasingly characterized my in-session behavior. Finally, I learned that I could say anything without fear of rejection.

At times, Hank reacted to "my verbal baloney." For example, during one session I was discussing my "failed life." His reply was unexpected: "You might as well drop this irrelevant self-descriptor. It's wasted breath and does you no good." On another occasion, I was carrying on about all the inadequacies of my father, and Hank, running out of patience, said, "All you do is bitch and waste time when you talk about your father. Why don't you just say you never liked him! I can accept that." I never did like my father and still don't, but up to that point, I had felt that I should. Hank's reaction to my bitching cut to the chase. I didn't realize that disliking my father was not so bad, nor was it unusual. Dr. Olivier's same reaction accompanied the haranguing episodes about Mother.

However, admitting that I didn't care for (nor love) either parent posed very serious problems for me. This realization or insight was to change my entire life, the course my life had taken up to this point and ultimately, the way I viewed myself. A cluster of issues surrounding the fact of not caring for or loving either parent, thrust me into a stark realization that I had never felt I had a mother or a father! This thunderous awareness brought down a ton of bricks on my head! Realizing the salience of strong negative feelings toward both parents was one thing; but when this insight unearthed the startling emotional emptiness and desolation that lay underneath all the anger and rage, my very psychological hold on sanity began to shake. Thinking back on these times in therapy still unnerves me.

I was confronted with a critical psychological problem. What do I do now once the abyss of emptiness and nothingness is exposed? Not only was I confronted with what seemed like a bottomless pit of emptiness,

I was also faced with the fact that I had never experienced many social feelings that normal growing up offers—that is, interpersonal trust, feelings of safety and self-confidence, and the social skills that accrue from these emotions.

These insights were closely followed by the frightening explicit emotional awareness that I had never felt loved or cared for. Next, I was hit with the alarming insight that this deep emotional emptiness left me with no viable emotional foundations to stand on or to construct a life with. The extent of this felt emptiness introduced me existentially to the abyss of terror—of nothingness and the calling into question everything that had provided a modicum of meaning. It sounds senseless to say as I pen this, but anger, rage, rejection and auto-eroticism had provided the only meanings I had experienced. Wiping these emotions off the table left me more alone than I had ever felt before. These insights also resulted in an avalanche of realizations: my life-long felt anger and rage, my misbehavior in elementary and junior high school and my avoidant social-interpersonal lifestyle masked an emotional emptiness that appeared right now to be unfathomable. I'd never thought that anger and rage could mask emotional emptiness. They were just the emotions I usually felt, but the tacit knowledge behind my hostility now became a frightening explicit type of knowledge. I faced the daunting and unanswered question: *Can a childhood predicament of this magnitude be resolved during adulthood? Is personal survival even possible for someone like me?* In the beginning, I had no answers for these questions, but over time, I realized that without Hank, I would not have dared move into such psychological territory. Perceptions like these are too frightening to confront alone.

My Turning Point in Psychotherapy. The first issue I faced was how could I insert a non-experienced emotional feeling in my life? How could I experience emotional feelings of trust and love when I had not felt these feelings before? I'm talking about *novel* emotional learning here! How can it happen?! Replacing my anger and rage with trust and love has been the most difficult challenge I've ever faced—a challenge that was to extend over the next fifty-eight years.

From this moment on, psychotherapy ceased to be a ventilation outlet for the perceived wrongs I'd received from others. Rather, it became a task of finding strategies to address the significant and inescapable emptiness arising from an awareness of a developmental history of emotional neglect and abuse.

My continued work with Hank provided clues. During one session, I realized the extent to which I felt interpersonally safe in these sessions. Though I had experienced his acceptance before, now, felt safety seemed different. Since the harangues and parental ventilations were largely behind me, the task had become now one of finding ways to put my life together. As I pondered further the experience of felt interpersonal safety, I realized that trusting Hank was something I was doing right now, in the present. So, I could experience a feeling of trust now that I had not felt before! I had my first demonstrable clue toward how to live in a healthier manner. *New learning was being actualized in the present within an interpersonal relationship of felt safety!* For me, the emotion of felt safety had to be experienced as an actual-reality-in-relationship. The experience was much more than just a cognitive fact or thought that I was told, heard about or read. This interpersonal experience of felt safety also required that time be spent with an accepting partner—felt safety is not quickly learned. In addition, I also realized there were several aspects involved in my experience of felt safety: (1) I first had to decrease my rage and anger toward persons who had hurt me; (2) then, I had to become aware of the relationship possibilities with Hank I was experiencing in the present; (3) finally, I needed to explore the relational possibilities that might exist on the outside with others.

Summarily, for the first twenty-four years of my life, I lived trusting very few persons outside the Binkley Group. Earlier and not surprisingly, I had kept myself at a safe interpersonal distance using various strategies such as misbehavior in school, breaking social rules among my peers and generally avoiding any physical or emotional challenges that threatened me. I also realized that emotional abuse and neglect had left a void in me that could only be filled with deliberate, sought-after interpersonal experiences designed to replace felt emptiness with trust. Preaching, lecturing, reading or mental exercises had little power to remedy or replace the earlier interpersonal realities of abuse and neglect. This is true because I was not able to cognitively persuade myself that life was good and people would care for me when earlier interpersonal realities persuaded me otherwise. The earlier lessons were too powerful and refractory to modify. I had to discover for myself within real-life relationships that these earlier negative realities of harm were just one of many possibilities that could be overcome when confronted with new interpersonal realities of felt safety. I had much catching up to do! I was also becoming increasingly aware that there was no blueprint or map for the road ahead. The trip would always be sluggish and full of novel forays into foreign interpersonal territories—one step at a time.

As noted above, once safety exists in a relationship, new interpersonal learning becomes possible. The reason for this is that fear drives and motivates interpersonal avoidance; hence, avoidance precludes the occurrence of new learning. I could never learn anything new as long as I backed off from challenging stressors. Once my generalized interpersonal avoidance was modified and replaced with felt safety, facing the challenges I once fled from opened the possibility of new intrapersonal learning. I knew the next step would be a difficult one.

Felt Helplessness and Self-rejection. I can recall lying awake at night while I was working with Hank and while at St. Luke's inundated in self-loathing.

The night periods were the worst. Thinking of the myriad ways my life was inadequate offered no real-life alternatives I could rely on. In actuality, there was nothing positive I could recall or focus on that I had accomplished. All previous memories led to hell, and these self-rejection episodes appeared fathomless and interminable. I'm reminded of the awful chambers of horror in Dante's *Inferno*—the suffering of the souls was endless. As noted above, when the realities of early developmental rejection have been actual and frequent, talking oneself into another reality-state is impossible—goodness knows I tried. The reason is that the data are in, the jury's decision has been made and the verdict is horrific and final since it was the only known interpersonal reality. Thus, I thrashed about in a sea of negativity surrounded with the sharks of rejection. During such times, I found *no exit* from these beasts. Then, the next healthfulness clue presented itself.

One evening when another episode of despair ensued, I thought of Hank and the accepting relationship we shared. Suddenly, the attacking sharks and the accompanying distress they represented vanished, and in their place, a calm self-acceptance emerged. This was the first time I'd actually escaped from the beasts who had dominated my life since I was a small boy. At first I couldn't believe what had happened. Stunned, I experienced a different emotional feeling where previously despair and anguish had predominated. Similar to my previous initial reaction to felt safety, I immediately connected the shift in emotions to the relationship I shared with Hank. Once again, the refractory and long-standing, negative emotion-state moved and shifted as a function of my new interpersonal relationship. Over time, I realized I had found the key to unlock the doors of confining emotion dungeons which had imprisoned me for years. What were required were new positive interpersonal relationships that must be added and which afforded a safe and stable attachment. These interpersonal additions could set me free to mature and to grow psychologically. Remember the questions I asked earlier? *Can a childhood predicament of this magnitude be resolved during adulthood? Is personal survival even possible for someone like me?* Now, I had my answers!

I cannot emphasize strongly enough the significance of the discovery of these critical formulas for growth. Numerous times throughout my life, particularly when I enter new relationships, the first response is usually fear and avoidance. These feelings are now countered by new emotional experiences described above as well as many new ones encountered since Hank and I finished our work. I am now convinced that interpersonal avoidance is, for me, the worst response I can make. Pushing past the initial negative reactions and pursuing the newness of encounter while being open to the growth that is offered is the only way to live. I have followed this formula for growth thousands of times in my life - my clinical career, particularly in my work with patients, during my marriage, raising three children and now during my retirement. The formula for growth has become my MANTRA for living:

PUSH PAST INTERPERSONAL AVOIDANCE;

PLUNGE INTO RELATIONSHIP;

LOOK FOR AVENUES OF PERSONAL GROWTH!

Career Choice Identification. I don't remember exactly when, but shortly after completing my work with Hank, I began to seriously consider leaving the parish ministry. At the time, I was in my third year at St. Luke's Methodist Church and becoming increasingly certain that the ministry was not what I wanted as a career. My therapeutic attachment to Dr. Olivier provided a clue regarding a career choice. I liked the manner in which he related to me and several other patients I knew about; I found his open style of response coupled with personal opinions compelling; and I admired his ability to be himself and to be able to push beyond a professional, one-way "doctor-patient role." Hank had taught me how to relate to other people. Looking back, my perception of his therapeutic goal with me was to teach me how to have a productive interpersonal relationship with Dr. Olivier—a relationship free of all the destructive trappings I'd learned from my previous maltreatment history. I wanted to be like him and work in a profession that afforded this possibility. Entry into medicine would entail completing several more years of undergraduate preparatory work, then, four years of medical school coupled with a year of internship and four additional years of residency training in psychiatry. This course of study would have put me into my late-thirties. Though this was one appealing alternative, the years it would take made this trajectory a discouraging one, not to mention the expenses that I couldn't pay given my monthly salary of $350. I began to explore the field of psychology and decided to enter the University of Georgia's (UGA) Clinical Psychology Training Program. I applied, was accepted and entered UGA in the fall, 1964, and I completed my Ph.D. in August, 1970. I graduated from UGA with the added and quite unexpected bonus of extensive training in research design and methodology in addition to the clinical patient training which, of course, was my first love.

I learned something else here with Hank in my career "identification strivings." I needed a specific model or roadmap to emulate when it came to making a career choice. Not knowing what I wanted to do with my life was directly related to the absence of an identifiable and significant attachment individual. I mentioned previously that I was psychologically adrift at age twenty-one when I completed LSU. Knowing what I wanted to do with my life was unattainable so I just enrolled in Perkins School of Theology because "I didn't know anything else to do." Working with Hank provided a definite and available attachment personage that I wanted to emulate. Dr. Olivier offered the pattern and made my choice of a career specific and doable—a very different *decision-situation* than the one I'd faced several years before.

Thirty-six Years Later. The last time I saw Hank was in 2001. I was lecturing at a psychological conference in New Orleans and drove ninety miles north to Baton Rouge to visit him. He was working at Charis Hospital, a substance abuse center in south Baton Rouge. During the visit, I presented Hank with my first CBASP book with a large 'THANKS' written and signed on the title page. I also told him that my second book was going to be published shortly and that I was dedicating it to him. He was overwhelmed, cried like a baby and kept saying, "Jimbo, Jimbo, Jimbo." He FAXED me shortly, writing, "I am overwhelmed by your kindness and generosity, both in the gift of your book and the intended dedication of your next. Rarely does one get to see the real fruits of one's labors in such a concrete fashion. Warmest regards, Hank." Because he died with an abdominal aortic aneurysm shortly before the second book was published in 2001, I dedicated it to him—"In Memory of Dr. Henry R. Olivier: My friend and first mentor."

Chapter Five:

Rosemary Fleming

Our relationship began in the Spring, 1963, during my second year as minister of St. Luke's Methodist Church. I'd been invited by the Wesley Foundation at LSU to lecture on the writings of a German theologian, Rudolf Bultmann. The occasion was the Wesley Foundation's annual retreat at Camp Singing Waters, a YMCA site outside Baton Rouge. I arrived around 2 P.M. on a Saturday. The college students were engaged in a rousing game of softball and playing on a dusty relic of a baseball field. I noticed a young lady who was bent over, beating a glove and shouting encouragement to the pitcher. She was playing second base. I was captivated by everything about this woman and thought at the time, "I've got to meet her." During my lecture, before I had a chance to introduce myself, she asked a question about the theologian. It was the one question of the lecture that I could not answer. I fumbled around with several attempts and finally admitted I was not sure what the answer was.

After the lecture, I walked up and introduced myself and we began to talk. She was from Dallas, Texas and was the most beautiful woman I had ever seen. We ate supper together and then sat next to each other during the worship service. I asked if I might call her during the week and she said, "Yes." It is fifty-six years later as I recall these memories. I can still feel the excitement of that moment. I did call and we went out on a date the next week. I picked up Rosie at her dormitory, South Hall, and we went to the Starmist Lounge on Nicholson Drive. We danced to a song that became a theme song of our relationship—Tony Bennett's "Blue Velvet". During one dance I kissed her on the left cheek. Little did I realize what I was getting into and what unforeseen emotions from my earlier years with my mother would present themselves. I was too caught up in the moment to even be aware of such matters and plunged ahead.

Rosie and I dated for the remainder of the spring semester, 1963, and she returned to Dallas in May for summer break. I didn't contact her during the summer. I was on the LSU campus the next fall and accidently ran into her. She angrily asked why I had vanished and not stayed in contact. I had little to say but probably made some sheepish excuse. The truth was that she was 'out of sight and out of mind.' My immaturity at maintaining a relationship was clearly obvious (to me) but she pressed on and asked if we were going to see each other again. I said I wanted to, and we began dating. Had she not taken the initiative and nudged me back into relationship, I would have ultimately lost the most precious individual who has ever graced my life. Thinking about that possibility now is still unnerving. Later on in the year while we were on a ferry crossing the Mississippi River, I asked her to marry me. She consented, and we were married in Dallas on January 17, 1964, at the University Park Methodist Church.

I don't know how to write what I'm about to say and make it understandable to the reader, but during the years that followed the wedding in 1964, I was beset by the demons that roamed the emotional landscape when I was growing up with my mother: emotional numbing, interpersonal isolation, a sense of loneliness, pervasive fear and a lack of trust, rage and a strong inner-push to emotionally withdraw—I was reeling from my own emotions and not dealing realistically with Rosemary. The experience was like a dark pall cast over me and my marriage. I couldn't escape it. To say that I didn't know how to maintain a conjugal relationship is putting it mildly. I had naively assumed that I had put to rest all the horrific emotions of childhood through my work with Hank—how wrong I was. These 'uninvited emotional invaders,' automatically and consciously, overran the marriage relationship. They threatened to break out and tear us apart. The unanticipated and negative emotions that suddenly erupted out of the depths of my psyche were comparable to someone unexpectedly throwing red paint over the Mona Lisa, or walking in The Tree of Life Synagogue in Pittsburgh on October 26, 2018, and murdering nine people. I experienced an *intrapersonal attack* against a person whom I thought I held to be dear and wonderful.

Thrust into a relational-threatening domain generated by my own demons, the only verbal expression that even begins to describe the horrible experience was a deeply felt despairing, "Aw shucks!" This self-reaction to my emotions was a familiar one: *I've really messed up again!* Was I prepared for marriage? No. Did I grow up in a home that modeled what a loving marriage was all about? No. What in the world did I think marriage was all about? Wasn't it just a man living with a woman and having sex? NO! Did I want to feel the negative emotions I was experiencing? No! No! No! I was faced with a foreign and novel interpersonal relationship while floating in waters that were shark-filled, and while stranded in a flimsy life raft with no paddle—and, there was no safe harbor in sight.

I resigned my ordination and left the Methodist ministry during the summer of 1964. Rosie and I moved from Baton Rouge and drove to

Athens, Georgia, where I entered clinical training at the University of Georgia (UGA). Prior to graduate training in clinical psychology, I had taken one introductory psychology course at LSU years before. My graduate colleagues in the program were all psychology majors for whom our first year was a review. This was not the case for me. Unexpectedly, Sigmund Freud, although certainly known in UGA academic circles, played a very minor role in this training program. This was surprising to me given my history with Dr. Hank Olivier, an analyst. I thought clinical psychology would be an extension of Freud's thought and work. Not so. Everything was novel! A new wife, the beginnings of a new career and a highly demanding coursework curriculum—this is what I had created for myself and Rosie. I had made the decisions and there was no going back to Louisiana. Again, how naïve I had been! I was a stranger in a foreign land in every living domain.

I was swimming upstream once more and staring at a six-year Ph.D. clinical training course. I couldn't blame anyone else for this dilemma. It was all my doing! Living through the first year at UGA was difficult and perhaps the hardest days I have ever had. I had no idea how my long-term decisions would come out, and the relationship with Hank Olivier and the new learning I had gleaned from him appeared to be several galaxies away.

How did I make it? It was not by accident. I did know several things that added stability to my otherwise storm-infested personal life. I had married a woman who loved me even though I knew little about what love was all about. Rosie was a generally optimistic person who was clever and resilient. I was also aware that I didn't want any part of the sterile marriage my parents had, though at the time, I had no idea how to make things different. I would have to learn to be a husband without any roadmap to guide me but with a help-mate who was solidly by my side. Secondly, I was determined to learn to be a clinical psychologist even though I realized each day that my expectations of the field were quite different from the actual reality; clinical psychology was *not* psychiatry. Third, I was determined to successfully play catch-up with my training colleagues who had a running start on me as far as academic preparation. Where did my courage to be come from? I'm not sure. During my first year at UGA, *I personally and deliberately refused to surrender to the demons.* I also knew that I was faced with an intrapersonal war that would be protracted and that somehow I must defeat the demons on all fronts if I was ever to learn to be a normal adult male.

It is always easier when current challenges are informed by past positive experiences that are similar to current realities. This was not to be my lot. Everything in clinical training and in my marriage was novel, so I put my nose to the grindstone beset by serious personal doubts and fears. As has been the case throughout our fifty-five-year marriage, Rosie was totally supportive. She also began working in the UGA Library and took a master's degree in French Literature during our fourth year in Athens in between the times she was cataloging books. Over the next few years, we socialized with eight couples in all sorts of activities from picnics to evening drinking bouts. Most of those marriages ended in divorce. We finished clinical training an intact couple and with a son who slept in a bassinette during my Ph.D. graduation exercises.

What were those six years in clinical training like? I was spending my days attempting to quell WWIII that was raging inside. I was feeling a great deal of fear and self-questioning as I went about my academic activities. The fears were omnipresent and became intimate and constant companions. I refused to give in to them and avoid novel situations. Significantly challenging in the curriculum was statistics. My colleagues had taken calculus and other higher order math courses in high school and undergraduate college. I had not. Statistics is grounded on the assumptions that earlier math courses impart (e.g., calculus). I remember one colleague during our first year who had previously been a chemical engineer before entering UGA's program. He worked the statistics examination problems on a slide rule. I was lost. I sought out a tutor to try to bring me up to speed but never felt I satisfactorily met criterion. My mathematical deficit has haunted me throughout my forty-seven-year clinical career and led to a feeling of inferiority whenever I compared myself to faculty colleagues, most of whom were mathematics experts. This was also the one area in my fourth year doctoral examinations I feared—my fear turned out to be realistic. Somehow, I passed that section of the exam in 1998 the second time I took my doctoral exams. The remainder of the subject matter in the clinical curriculum was not difficult; in fact, I did well in other courses and functioned adequately with patients in the applied clinical arena.

I learned one thing about myself over the six years I was in training. I learned I was hard-wired with a personality trait—*perseverance*. Sticking with my goals and seeing them through to completion enabled me to maintain a marriage under the worst invasion of personal emotions imaginable and facilitated my success in the training program and in a clinical career of forty-seven years.

My Quietly Troubled Marriage. When I began clinical training in September, 1964, I was an internal or intrapersonal "divided house." On the outside, I studied hard, attended classes, wrote term papers, passed exams and tried to be a considerate husband. On the inside, I was terrified by the "foreign" emotional territory I was in and of the inadequacies I felt that called into question everything I did. Trying to maintain some semblance of order on the outside and in the marriage took most of my psychological energy.

What was it like? It was my childhood all over again, only this time I was a twenty-seven-year-old adult! Emotionally, I was back home and feeling like a small boy with all my self-doubts, self-recriminations and all the while, emotionally connected to my mother but sleeping with a new wife. I had resolved many of the issues with my father through work with Hank, but not with my mother. Marriage also presented an additional issue I had not anticipated. Never having lived in a harmonious household with two loving parents, I found myself engulfed by earlier divisive feelings between Rosie and other males that tore at my insides and gave me considerable pain: *I could not resolve the former divisions I experienced which were pulling me in two directions between a possessive mother and jealous-enraged father.* What do I mean here? I found myself caught between my relationships with male peers and Rosemary. Most of my early years at UGA, I was always pulled in two directions. I didn't know emotionally how to be attached to and comfortable with male friends while at the same time be attached to and comfortable with Rosemary. Emotionally it had to be one or the other—the way it had always been growing up. To put it bluntly, I had no clue how to care for more than one person at a time or to attach emotionally with two different people simultaneously. When I was younger, I never thought about this as an important issue. I just experienced the inner emotional conflict that involved me and two parents. It was either one or the other.

The way I reacted to my mother much of the time was to feel nothing; it was an emotional numbing experience. I could be in her presence yet feel emotionally barren. I also experienced these depersonalization episodes in elementary, middle and high school when with female teachers. I could misbehave and knowingly be a source of considerable stress to my teachers, yet feel nothing emotionally. Without being able to experience love or caring toward others, the barrenness of affect was a genuine source of distress; I would know I had done something wrong, but the appropriate emotions were absent. Interpersonal empathy toward others or caring about what I had done to others was an emotional ability that was poorly developed in junior high and high school. The experience of interpersonal depersonalization returned in my early marriage and much of the time during our first years I felt emotionally numb around Rosie. The experience was familiar and unnerving. I behaved on the outside as a dutiful husband yet felt like a robot on the inside. I could still feel sexual arousal, but little else. In the nothingness-emotional arena, what I did experience was fear, interpersonal isolation and dread. At times, I would become furious at my emotional inadequacy but the anger and rage led to no resolution. Even as I write about these emotional memories now, I become enraged. The truth was that my emotional capacities were severely constricted. Readers may shake their heads in confusion. At the time, so did I.

The price early emotional chaos exacts and the outstanding debt emotional chaos requires must be paid in full with emotional resolution and change before one's life can achieve any semblance of normalcy. How would I learn emotional maturity when I had never experienced it? How would I learn what the vast majority of people learn as children and never think twice about? This was the serious affectual dilemma I faced.

There was one thing I became increasingly aware of during the early years at UGA. The woman I married was not going to leave me and she continuously affirmed my efforts at study and within our relationship. I shared at length the earlier struggles with my mother and father, and Rosemary became excruciatingly cognizant of my difficulties making discriminations between her and Mother. You would think that she would finally tell me she'd had enough and leave, but not this lady. As with Hank, I kept getting daily reminders that I was accepted in spite of my stupid, immature baloney.

One example happened at the supper table during our second year in Athens. She and I moved from an apartment to a four-room country house on a large piece of land with a two-acre pond situated behind the little house. We paid Mr. Shackleford, who liked to rent his house to UGA graduate students, fifty dollars a month. The pond was filled with largemouth bass and had a wooden rowboat tied to the bank—lucky for us as we had little money left over for food. I always freshwater fished as a younger boy and had brought my fishing equipment to UGA. I loved to fly fish and, on many afternoons, would take my fly-rod and row out on the water and catch several bass. In those days, we had very little spending money so the fried fish, the delicious hushpuppies she made along with her tossed salads provided tasty eating. While we were eating one evening, Rosie said to me, *"It takes a man to provide the meal for our dinner."* The initial shock was that I was living with a woman who thought of me as a man! This was a first of many such shocks. As with Hank, I gradually realized that my first anticipated rejections and criticisms never came; instead, her affirmations of me were frequently verbalized. Over time, and it took time, compare and contrast discriminations between Rosie and my mother undercut the strength of the older negative expectations and emotions I felt as a boy. I would often lie awake at night and think about these types of events while looking at Rosemary gently sleeping by my side and quietly say under my breath, *"I'm really not sleeping with my mother! Thank God!"*

I recall one unfortunate experience that occurred at my parents' home in Shreveport when Rosie and I visited them before I graduated. At the time, she and I had been married about five years. We had just arrived driving from Athens, Georgia to Shreveport, Louisiana—a trip of about 670 miles. The evening was wintry-cold. I had unpacked the car when my father started in on me. He told me I must go lock my car to prevent theft. I didn't want to go back outside in the cold and told him so. He wouldn't quit haranguing me in his hostile manner. Rosie was a bit surprised by the encounter—it was about the two thousandth round for me. As usual, a small issue was evolving into a major crisis. I was not going to go back outside. He continued his lecture about thefts in the neighborhood while repeatedly demanding that I lock the car. After several of his heated comments, I lost my temper. I got very close to his face and told him that if he mentioned my car again, I was going to deck him and lay him out on the floor. He withdrew at this point, went upstairs and said no more. In fact, he never spoke or communicated with me again for two years. I was embarrassed that Rosemary had to witness this confrontation, but she was well aware of the problems in our relationship. At that point, my mother reacted with her traditional heaving sigh over the present chaos of the evening and apologized to Rosie for the conflict. We went to bed. I remained mad.

Gradually during the waning days at UGA, the warm emotions of care and love that I felt during the early days of our relationship slowly began to return. As with Hank, interpersonal *felt-safety* and *trust* was evolving with Rosie in that I came to believe that she would never emotionally abandon me nor try to hurt me. In contrast, I never trusted that my mother would not abandon or hurt me. This was an important emotional discrimination that gave me hope. I'm sure my mother would not have understood what I am writing here because I never experienced such feelings of felt-safety with her. I was awakening to the fact that I had found another unexpected and novel emotional event. The older formula for growth mantra that I learned from Dr. Olivier was again validated:

PUSH PAST INTERPERSONAL AVOIDANCE;

PLUNGE INTO RELATIONSHIP;

LOOK FOR AVENUES OF PERSONAL GROWTH!

Dr. William K. Boardman. While these emotional changes were ongoing between Rosie and me, I began working on research with a major clinical professor, William K. Boardman. The work entailed a program of research that would ultimately lead to the completion of my doctoral dissertation. A characteristic that attracted me to Bill Boardman was that he was an avid hunter and fisherman. He knew more about the former than the latter. We hunted dove and quail and fished for rainbow trout and largemouth bass in several of the pristine streams in north Georgia. Bill bought a 16-foot polyurethane bass boat which significantly facilitated our outdoor efforts during my last two years at UGA. In addition to my program of research, we discussed hunting and fishing constantly.

Once again, and not surprisingly, I entered the interpersonal relationship with Dr. Boardman in fear and trembling. The older habits die hard. Here was a senior clinical faculty member whom I respected but remained wary of. What if I failed to meet his expectations with research? What if my proposed experimental dissertation design was inadequate? What if I took too long to do the research, and he grew weary working with me? What if, what if, what if, etc.? I was thinking back from failed end-goals from an earlier time and always saw myself coming up short. This was the first time I had undertaken research that was my own and, as I considered the challenge, I expected to fail. As my past experience had demonstrated with Hank and Rosie, I again found Bill to be supportive of the research program throughout and a working relationship of felt safety between us evolved. He liked what I was doing and frequently reminded me of this. Being able to discriminate between earlier toxic players in my life and current significant others paved the way for me to experience productive outcomes. My persistent march toward mental health continued.

Over the more than two years I worked with Bill, Rosie and I spent time visiting in his home. We attended parties that Bill and his wife, Katie, gave, ate meals in their home and of course, he and I spent time hunting and fishing. Both Katie and Bill liked and admired Rosemary. Another discovery I experienced in my interactions with this couple was that I had married someone who garnered respect from both of them. This may sound trivial to one who had grown up in a positive and nurturing environment, but to one who came from a home where nothing he did was considered valuable or worthy of respect, this was a significant discovery. Bill often visited in our home, and he and I would proofread the countless dissertation pages I typed. In those days before the advent of computers, we would review the pages I had typed on a Royal typewriter. If I made a mistake and could not erase the error (no white-out in 1968), the page had to be retyped. There was no such thing as a deletion, nor could I add sentences or move paragraphs around without retyping pages. Writing a dissertation or publishing a paper was an arduous process prior to the word processor. Pulling the final manuscript together became a joint effort between the two of us and culminated in 1969 in a successful dissertation defense with my doctoral dissertation committee.

I graduated from UGA in August, 1970, credentialed as a clinical psychologist and with a productive relationship with Dr. Boardman. Rosemary supported me throughout the years of clinical training and was immensely happy and proud over my accomplishments. The relationship I had with Bill was an optimal achievement—particularly being the case in graduate school. Again, and unexpectedly, I learned that while with Bill I could experience many of the gentle emotions I felt toward Rosie, while feeling simultaneously an enduring respect and admiration toward him. It became clear to me that becoming a mature human being requires that one is intimately connected with other mature individuals. It is an experience that must be lived out. It cannot be scripted or learned from reading books.

I was truly growing up, maturing and overcoming the early divisive affectual roadblocks that stunted and derailed my interpersonal growth. During my early professional years as a faculty member at the University of Southern Mississippi (two years) and Virginia Commonwealth

University, Bill and I continued to remain in touch. In 1975, we met in Shreveport, Louisiana, and traveled together by rental car to a large lake, Toledo Bend Reservoir. Toledo Bend was located on the dividing line between Louisiana and Texas. Some years earlier, damning up the Sabine River by the Corp of Engineers created the reservoir with its 1,200 miles of shoreline. The reservoir had acquired a reputation for excellent largemouth bass fishing by the early 1970s. We hired a guide for the day and the three of us went bass hunting. We had a day that could be called nothing short of a "Field and Stream Day" (to use the magazine title as a descriptor) as we caught over 110 bass using plastic worms on 20-pound test lines. Many of these fish weighed over 4 pounds. Reliving the old UGA days and discussing my career at VCU filled the day. Bill knew of my experiences with Dr. Olivier and the motivation to be a psychotherapist I had that led to my entering clinical training. He respected my decision to become a clinician. He also encouraged me to continue doing patient-research, especially if I wanted to remain a university faculty member. He mentioned several times that I was one of the few *"research-practitioners"* that had matriculated out of the UGA clinical training program. Most of my clinical colleagues had become either university faculty members and quit treating patients, or they had entered into private practice with little involvement in research-related work. Bill was proud that I was doing both types of work in my career. Our relationship was a wonderful experience that brought huge personal dividends to my life and it was qualitatively different compared to what I had experienced years earlier. While I was to draw strength from our relationship throughout my life, Bill died in 1978.

I received a call from Katie one afternoon that Bill had been killed in a car accident in Athens while driving back to the university campus after lunch. He was fifty-three years old and at the height of his clinical career as the program director of the UGA Clinical Training Program in the Department of Psychology. Sadly, I traveled to Athens, Georgia, for the funeral and buried the second mentor and personal friend I had had. How many times over the years I've wanted to pick up the phone and tell him what I was doing or disclose some award or grant I had just received. I'm certain he would have been very proud. Of course, this was not possible; instead, I was left with his significant and abiding legacy to my life as a *mentor and personal friend.* Hank and Bill assisted me to mature in many ways. What I take from both those relationships is an endearing sense of gratitude for what they gave me.

A Maturing Marriage. How can I adequately express what I learned from living with Rosie during the years I was at UGA? One way to make explicit these lessons is to compare and contrast her to my mother. Once again, new learning occurs in situations similar to earlier ones when the major player responds to one in different ways. This happened in my intimate exchanges with Rosemary.

She exposed me to an interpersonal relationship of felt safety through her continuous love and acceptance. My mother confronted me with felt danger through her dominant, protective and overwhelming parenting. With Rosie, I felt affirmed and courageous. Conversely, my mother rendered me inadequate and socially isolated from peers and adults. With Rosie I felt I could be a strong male while mother punished me in subtle and not so subtle ways for manly pursuits and emotions. I respected Rosie and her many strengths around others. I was embarrassed to be around my mother in social situations because she was loud, aggressive and at times, rude to others. Rosie was empathically gentle in our relationship. I don't think my mother had an empathic bone in her body. At times I thought of my mother as more masculine than feminine because of her aggressive behavior and mannerisms toward others. Rosie, on the other hand, was feminine and soft in everything she did and for the first time, taught me who and what a woman is. I trusted Rosie because she was consistently available and loving to me interpersonally. I never trusted my mother because I never knew whether she would be emotionally present or absent. I feared her disapproval as well as her emotional absence. Rosie was a risk-taker and actively pursued what she wanted professionally; she usually obtained it. Mother was not. She was a fearful individual who generally withdrew from interpersonal conflict particularly where anger was involved.

Rosie always listened to me and respected what I said. Mother did not and she was not often influenced by what I wanted or didn't want; being around her was living with someone who usually did exactly what she wanted to do. For example, if I came home from college and left my suitcase at the bottom of the stairs asking that it remain there while I got some water from the kitchen, I would come back and she, not my father, would have taken my suitcase upstairs. On trips home during my undergraduate days, she fixed breakfast and never asked what I wanted—it was always her menu even though I might not even want anything but coffee. This led to contentious conflicts between us most of which were irrelevant and went nowhere. In face of her interpersonal onslaughts, I had the frequent inner feeling while in her presence of "not existing."

I always felt that Rosie loved me even in the early days of our marriage when I hardly felt anything but a generalized state of emotional numbing. I never felt that my mother loved me. I'm not sure what she felt, but it was not what I have learned to feel with Rosemary. As I mentioned earlier, my father died palpably angry with Mother. She had chastised him for going to sleep during numerous social occasions in the last months of his life—his progressive heart failure was increasingly interfering with his daily functioning. While he lived out his last two weeks in the ICU, he refused to speak to her—it was pay-back time! They were married forty-eight years and the relationship ended in a stand-off. I never knew how they really felt toward each other, nor did I ever see them kiss, embrace or hold hands. Her later memories of their marriage which she repeatedly described sounded like something out of a romantic Hollywood movie. I never observed those endearing and loving relationship qualities while my father was alive.

Summarily, Rosie is everything that my mother was not. I am not over-stating my case—I have literally learned to be a human being living with her. She wrote a recent Prayer (July 2018) about us that I've copied below. I've included it because it captures the way she views me and illustrates the type of relationship we have built over fifty-five years. It clearly does not reflect how I began the marriage, but it describes us now.

Dear God: Thank you for Jim. Thank you for the love he has for me and for our children. Thank you for his brain, which is so amazing, and smart. Thank you for the way he has used his brain to help so many people. Help him use his wonderful brain to find more peace for him-self. Thank you for his hands, which do so many things to help me take care of our home, yard and cars. Thank you for his willingness to get help for some things that we can't do and for the way he manages these helpers. Thank you for his arms, which hold and caress me. Thank you for the ways he loves me and cherishes me. Help him to take in the ways I love him. Thank you for the ways he lets me help him take on the new demands of his body. Help us work together smoothly. Amen.

Chapter Six:

Becoming a Father without Having Had a Father

At the outset of a journey, not knowing where one is going is nonsensical. When my first son was born in 1970, I was thirty-four years old and had no idea how to be a father. I had no roadmap for "fatherhood" from my earlier home-life nor did I have a clue concerning the best paternal road to take with Michael. Again and as in so many other situations I've described, the parental trajectory that lay before me was strange territory. And once more, I feared the worst outcomes imaginable. However, I did have three tools available that provided me some modicum of hope. The first was my accepting helpmate of a wife. I was confident that I could always count on her help and support. Secondly, I had taken a series of early-childhood developmental courses in the clinical training program that described how the "optimal male parenting role" should be lived out. I learned some things to do and certainly some things to avoid. Lastly, I decided on a standard of parenting that I would to try to live by: *whatever my father did with me, I would do the opposite with Mike*. I followed this negative rule-of-thumb throughout my parenting days up to and including the present time. It has served me well. I must mention, however, that this standard was based on an intellectual decision and was not emotionally grounded. I quickly learned that the old emotional roadblocks and habits arose reflexively while parenting Mike and, when present, had to be aggressively attacked and rejected. My early emotional legacy from my father remained a stubborn beast that I had to defeat if I was to be a good father. The specific motivation to be a good father was strong and has remained a high priority life-goal. I was determined to avoid recreating the parental disasters I had lived through. The first challenge was to enact a non-avoidance interpersonal style with my son.

The Interpersonal Absence of My Father. One legacy I inherited from my father was his almost total interpersonal absence. He remained a true "phantom"—withdrawn, detached and avoidant. The most prominent memories I have of him involve his verbal and nonverbal tirades which usually occurred during the evening hours. At other times, he was not available interpersonally in any facilitative way. When I played or practiced baseball or basketball or when I played in high school golf tournaments, he never came. I don't recall him ever wanting to talk to me about anything or seeking me out to be with me. He was not interpersonally present for conversations when I needed to discuss issues or problems I was having at school; he never inquired how I was doing or what I was doing. The result was that I never learned how to talk with him. He never offered a hand when I had difficult homework assignments. He never offered encouragement when I faced challenges with peers, teachers or coaches. As mentioned earlier, I never heard him say one word of praise or congratulations to me for anything I ever did. I never knew what it was like to see him manage difficult situations for he was never around nor shared anything about what was ongoing in his life. At eighteen, when I left for college in Baton Rouge, he never wrote nor seemed interested in how or what I was doing. He never inquired about any of my career issues nor was he curious about what I wanted to do with my life. When I ran for student body president at LSU, which I lost by just a few votes, he never tried to find out how the campaign was going or called to see how I was after losing a tough race. When I left for Perkins School of Theology after my LSU graduation, he never said anything about my decision to go to Perkins. When I married and asked him to be my best man and requested his comments at the rehearsal dinner, he never said anything nor was he any help to me with the marriage process—clearly, he was not a "best man." He just stood around, was nice and sociable with others and left me alone. When I exited the church with Rosie after the ceremony and had my car "jacked up" and my keys stolen and thrown in the snow, he did nothing but stand in the back of the wedding group. All these omissions of his presence left me never knowing what it was like to have a father. He was no help to me nor did I ever feel that he had my back. Other than his anger, he remained the "shadow."

In summary, my father never existed to me in any facilitative or nurturing way. What I do recall when I think of him now is a perceptive miasma of nothingness. This vacuous emotional legacy haunted me for many years. I never knew who he really was other than he was always mad about something. He never liked the President of our country, the coaches at LSU whom he fussed about constantly nor what was happening in Shreveport or in the Louisiana state government. Frankly, I never heard him say he liked or enjoyed anything.

On one rare occasion and I don't recall what the situation was, he told me that his father was a "drunk," always angry, and an incompetent man who could never hold a job. My paternal grandfather's family remained dirt poor throughout my father's life. He also said that my great-grandfather was like that also and as far as he had heard, the tradition of incompetent fathers went back five generations in the McCullough family (all the way back to the Civil War). Why he told me all this, I never knew. But, this was the toxic legacy of fathers and sons on my father's side of the family that I inherited and that I was determined to put a stop to—*and I did with my children, Mike, John and Kristin!*

Raising Two Sons and a Daughter. Rosemary knew how to be a mother—thank goodness! She was the oldest sibling and had three younger brothers. Her mother recruited her early and taught her to help raise all three brothers. What a godsend legacy this became for us. She knew what to do. I certainly didn't. Rosie nursed all three of our children during the first year of their lives. She nursed them in the first piece of furniture we bought, an early English style rocking chair. That rocking chair cost fifty dollars. I was working at Farmer's Furniture Store in Athens at the time and purchased the chair for one third its cost. We still have the chair in our bedroom today—it's been refinished now with a French provincial stain and new padding and with a soft white skirt at the bottom. I learned quickly how to change diapers and since these were the 'ole days'—how to put the dirty cotton diapers in the pail that Rosie positioned next to the toilet. I was working on my dissertation at the time and was also a staff member in one of the adult units at Georgia Regional Hospital at Atlanta. When I came home from work in the afternoons, I would take Mike on long walks and feel very proud as I walked the neighborhood with him with his warm little head on my shoulder. I kept thinking, "My son and I. My son and I." At first, the reality of what was happening was unreal but that soon changed. An emotional bond developed that became progressively stronger over the years. Comparisons between what happened between Mike and me and my earlier years in Shreveport with my father stretch my imagination. The events on these afternoon walks as I felt Mike's little head on my shoulder were quiet, serene, and meaningful while my earlier years as I remembered them with my father had been chaotic, loud and frightening. Mike was so little, so warm and light in my arms. I couldn't remember a time when my father ever carried me or we walked hand-in-hand. I've never understood the demons he must have experienced that drove him to behave as he did. But, these days with Michael were different and would always remain so. Interestingly, while the present time with my son was different, I never forgot the toxicity of the past nor the pain and hurt that remained. As I behaved differently with Mike and my other two children, these small acts of kindnesses remained a constant reminder that I never received any of these generosities growing up. I gave my children what I never received—*ex nihilo*. My life goal had become to make certain I didn't repeat the past. This desired outcome remained one of the major aims of my adult life.

John was born two years later and then Kristin two years after that. I continued to discover new things about being a father. One concern I had before John was born was how would I be able to love him the way I loved Mike? How can one's heart expand to take in more than one person to love? This may sound quite trivial, but to me it was a genuine concern and the experience foreign. Quite surprisingly, once John was born, my heart embraced him and what I thought was going to be a problem was not. Isn't it strange that if one has not had certain precedent experiences like loving several persons concomitantly, the brain cannot generate an understanding of how this is possible? It just happened and what a relief to me that it did. The same repetitious discovery occurred when our third child was born. The heart's capacity to love must be quite infinite. In normal developmental trajectories, so much happens to growing children that are never considered later in life. They learn to trust, to expect help and support and to love their siblings, and they never think about how it all automatically emerges. To me, most everything was a novel experience, and I was acutely aware of these novelties all along the way. Given my history, I don't take the good things that come my way for granted.

John was born quickly and on the way to the delivery room, Rosie's Ob/Gyn physician and his nurse came down the hall pushing her gurney and stopping when they saw me. The doctor was a bass fisherman too. He and I began talking about a new bass lure that had just hit the stores. Rosie was quite uncomfortable at that time and could have cared less about fishing. She exclaimed loudly saying something like, "If you two don't quit talking, I'm going to have this baby in the hall!" We never completed the conversation.

Kristin was born in the morning and I slept through the delivery. Rosie's water broke early one morning on December 14, 1974, and we both drove to the hospital at 6 A.M. I was determined to stay awake for the delivery but fell asleep in the waiting room. I woke up with a start and rushed to the nurses' station to find out what happened. Taken by one of the nurses to her room, I walked in and she was holding our newest baby with the biggest smile I have ever seen on her face; she said, "We've got a girl!" Today, most couples know the sex of the child soon after the pregnancy is known - not so in the early 1970s. We never knew the sex of our child until after the delivery event. What a joyous surprise. Once again, I was in a new land with three very young children.

I discovered something else with our third child. For the first time since Michael's birth, Rosie and I were outnumbered. This became apparent whenever we went shopping or made weekly trips to the grocery store. One child was always loose and roaming. Rosie would have one in her cart and the second would be in mine—this meant that Michael would be free and loose. Most of the time, he walked with us, but not infrequently, while we were deciding whether to buy steak or sliced ham or some other food product, he'd wander off. We'd suddenly realize that we'd lost Michael! What aisle was he in? My task was to find the lost child while Rosemary stood guard over the two carts. The job of replacing cans of peas on the shelf or putting bags of Fritos back on a rack usually followed the discovery of the lost boy.

Our Children's Needs. The needs were small at first but become greater as the children aged. As I recall, when I was very young, my mother looked after my needs such as what clothes I was going to wear to school and when and what food I would eat. She saw that I had lunch money for the school cafeteria and helped me gather my books for the day. I don't remember my father helping with clothes or assisting my preparations for school. All I can remember about our daily morning routines was his getting dressed, eating breakfast and leaving with a colleague who picked him up for work. There was no talk about what was happening that day nor did I ever have any awareness of what he was doing or what my mother was going to do that day.

In comparison, our home was a bundle of activity in the morning. I was aware of what our children were going to do that school day and whether or not they had done their homework; then, it was my job to walk them to the corner to the school bus. During one year, our next door neighbor had a German shepherd dog he let run loose. Our children were afraid of the dog. The neighbor and I had several run-ins until he penned his dog up. Having my children's back or dealing seriously with their fear of the dog was uppermost in my mind.

Our second son, John, wrestled in middle school. The night before his first tournament, he was frightened over the day's match and couldn't sleep. I spent most of the night sitting in a chair next to his bed. Neither one of us got much sleep. Regrettably, he lost the match, but he did face his fear and complete the match. He and I have had some interesting experiences together. Both of us loved to fish and spent many hours in a bass boat on the lake. Once when John was about eleven years-old, we fished in a private three-acre pond stocked with fish using a twelve-foot Jon boat. We moved it around using a small "beaver" paddle. The owner of the pond was a friend. He told me that he had a dog that he let stay outside his country house. He said the dog, Molly, would probably not bother us but sometimes she became upset with visitors and barked—not to worry, he said.

We parked the car by the side of the house, picked up our tackle box, boat cushions, water jug, paddles and fishing rods and took the equipment down the hill where the boat was stowed. It took two trips down to get all the equipment in the boat. Molly passively watched us unload and appeared disinterested. We had a good day fishing—never caught anything over one pound but had lots of fun. We came back to the dock several hours later and tied the boat up. I told John I would make the first trip up and take some of the gear to the car while he put all lures in the tackle box and broke down the rods. I started up the hill to the house. Molly hit me halfway up the hill. The owner was right. She barked, and that day Molly tried to do much more. Luckily, I had brought the small paddle and boat cushions on the trip up and when she lunged at my legs, I fended her off with the cushions draped over an arm and pushed her back with the paddle in my other hand. This only enraged Molly. I yelled to John to stay in the boat, and I would be back for him in a moment. Getting some of our gear in the car while holding off the charging dog was dicey, but I managed to do so and avoid being bitten. Starting back down to the car, I took the two boat cushions and the paddle. Molly worked hard to get at my legs and when I got about halfway, she backed off and returned to the house. We worked out a strategy to get the remainder of the gear to the car. Halfway up the path, Molly or Cujo, rushed at us again - more vicious than ever. John had one boat cushion and I held the other. We were positioned butt-to-butt and using the cushions to keep the dog at bay, we rotated in a circular manner up the path fending off the charging dog while she kept looking for an opening. John would swat the dog with a rod while I used my small paddle. Neither worked very well but at least she couldn't get to our legs. Molly became even more frantic when we got to the car. I kept pushing her away while John threw our gear in the back seat and jumped in the car. This left me alone with Molly. It was one boat cushion and one small wooden paddle against an angry dog who really wanted a chunk of my leg. The irony of this tale is that I could have killed Molly with the paddle, but then I would have had to explain to my friend why I killed her which I didn't want to do. John opened my door, pulled the paddle in while I backed in blocking my legs with the cushion. I jumped in and closed the door. Mission accomplished! We were both safe in the car panting heavily, the doors were locked and Cujo was still jumping up on my side of the car. Shortly after our fishing trip to the pond, my friend called and asked how the day turned out. I thanked him for the use of his pond, told him we enjoyed the fishing but never mentioned Molly. A month later he called and said that Molly had been hit by a train crossing the train trestle that ran in front of his house. I suppressed a chuckle and expressed my condolences. John and I have had several experiences similar to this one on lakes in Virginia such as being lost in a fog on a large lake and caught in a lightning storm in a metal boat, but never one as harried as the Molly encounter.

Encounters like these generate deep attachments between fathers and sons and this was the case between John and me. John never knew it until much later, but his ole-man was engaging in totally new interpersonal experiences as a father. At eleven years old, what happened to us, though endearing, would have been unthinkable for me at his age—it would never have happened.

When my oldest son, Mike, was eleven years old, he and I visited some relatives in Lafayette, Louisiana, a middle-sized town west of Baton Rouge. We went crappie fishing with my uncle in one of the many bayous that populated the swamps around Lafayette. My uncle and my son,

John, were in one boat and Mike and I were in the other. Our small motor stopped running. I removed the three-horsepower motor from the stern and began repairing the carburetor. Mike was sitting in the front of the boat and I was in the back with the motor resting on my lap. It was the middle of the day and the noon sun was heating up the water as well as our metal twelve-foot Jon boat. Out of the blue, Mike made a comment that stunned me. He said something like, "You know, Dad, you really know how to do a lot of things." From that day on our relationship changed, and we became "comrades" in a way that was qualitatively different compared to earlier times—mutual respect became prominent.

Mike played basketball in high school. He had his sights during his junior year on making the varsity squad. He had played junior varsity the year before. At the designated morning, his coach posted the names of those who made the varsity on the gym bulletin board. I asked Mike to call me when he got to school and checked the list. He did. His name was not on the list. About 10 A.M., I went to the Freeman High School office and called him out of class. He checked out of school and we drove a long way up I-95 to Washington, DC. For a time, neither of us said anything. I finally said something like, "Mike, I'm really sorry. I just wanted to be with you today." We ended up spending the day together, not saying a lot, but just being together. He has said several times since that difficult day, how much being with me meant to him. Again, I adhered to the "game plan" I devised many years before and did with Mike what my father would never have done with me. The plan worked perfectly and over the years, it has produced relationships between me and all three children that have been robust and long-lasting.

Kristin had a particularly difficult time in the fourth grade, and it was obvious to me that most of the stress stemmed from her teacher whose general behavior in the classroom indicated that she shouldn't have been teaching elementary-aged children. She resigned at the end of the year and began selling real estate. Kristin would go to school, but attending class became increasingly distressful as her fourth year progressed. About once a week, I would go by her class and call her out just to see her, talk and offer a word of encouragement. Her teacher was obviously not pleased with my visits. My behavior contrasted to my experiences in the elementary grades; no one came by any class I had to see how I was doing. The only attention I ever received from my parents was negative attention due to in-class misbehavior.

The summer that Kristin was thirteen, she returned from a one-week vacation babysitting two small children whose parents had taken them to the beach. She was a changed person and we couldn't figure out what had happened. Her days and nights were reversed, meaning that she would not sleep at night but wanted to sleep all day. In the mornings, she would hide in the house to keep from going to school. She kept losing her gym clothes in her locker at school, and defiantly refused to dress-out during gym periods. Her behavior became erratic around the house, and our home became a 'battle ground' between herself and my wife. The chaotic state in our home became so extreme that we finally withdrew her from school, and she began an extended period of county home-instruction. Neither Rosie nor I had any idea what was going on with our daughter. Suddenly and without any forewarning, the world turned into a conundrum in the family as Rosie and I struggled to make sense of her extreme behavior changes. We met with her teachers, her guidance counselor, and I even visited one of her friends for answers. None came.

Finally, I received a call from a friend who asked if she could come by my office to talk and that time was of the essence. I met with her later that afternoon. She told me what the mother of one of Kristin's friends had confided to her: Kristin had been raped two years before while at the beach. I cancelled several appointments and picked up Rosemary, and we parked and talked near the house. I related what I had learned. We then began a six-year odyssey with Post Traumatic Stress Disorder (PTSD). Rosie's reaction to the rape was different from my reaction. She was *significantly relieved* to know what had happened because now we knew what we were dealing with and could get help. I became *intensely angry* and succumbed to a PTSD reaction that lasted approximately one year. During the year I had intense homicidal feelings that accompanied flashbacks of her rape. I exerted considerable self-control to reign in these homicidal urges, particularly when I was driving the car to and from work. The urges were to kill someone with my car. Since there was no object to my rage nor anyone to attach the anger to, the feelings remained indefinite and "free-floating"—which made it all the more difficult to control. I recognized that my stress reaction was related to my daughter's course of healing. When she had good days, I felt better. When she didn't, I felt worse. Two thoughts dominated my mind during this period: *I must take care of my daughter* and *I must try to make up to her for what has happened.* The former goal was doable, and I did all I could to help her out in every way possible. The latter she ultimately had to do for herself, but at the time I didn't see it that way. In my mind I felt that I must do something to make up for the catastrophe that had happened.

Healing. She and I watched TV together, particularly the Los Angeles Lakers play their yearly series with the Chicago Bulls. We talked together as never before, sharing and discussing what had happened to both of us. I learned during these times that she was very smart, courageous, resilient and best of all, determined to get back on her feet. Without ever denying the terrible events of that evening and its sequela, Kristin created a productive life for herself. She graduated with an undergraduate degree in biology, went through further training, married a wonderful man and has maintained a stable and loving marriage for nine years. The empathy she has for persons in distress in her medical field is evident today.

Recalling all this as I write has been difficult and left me feeling very uncomfortable. I am most grateful, however, for the fact that she has done so well and is such a loving and beautiful person. The events surrounding the trauma event were god-awful but not ultimately defining. In summary, she too has had to swim upstream, but Kristin has successfully completed the swim and produced huge rewards during the process.

Overall, becoming a father has been a difficult, satisfying and, in general, rewarding experience. With no roadmap, I was able to carve out a way to love and nurture all three children. I did it in different ways for their different needs. But always, I kept in mind the desired outcome goal I set when I became a father; that is, not to replicate the interpersonal damage my father inflicted on me. Looking back now, my desired outcome for becoming a father was realized.

Chapter Seven:

My Continuing Struggles over the Years

I wish I could write that my adult days have been smooth sailing ever since my work with Hank and during my marriage to Rosemary. This has not been the case. I have had to face new and difficult emotional challenges periodically and confront these episodes with proactive coping strategies. My first impulse, as I've noted above, is to avoid stress situations. Coping entails examining each challenging reality with its concomitant negative emotional reactions, then, using the skills I've learned while drawing strength from the supportive relationships which sustain me, I must decide what my desired outcome is to resolve the stress. The process of working my way through avoidance to get to risk-taking has been a never-ending process, though it's become easier over time. The old emotional learning still waits 'in the wings,' and the early neural connections laid down from maltreatment remain complicated and pervasive. But, I have learned through experience that I don't have to start over from the beginning every time. Examples of some of the difficult events I've faced involve children issues, encounters with Rosemary, facing some problem that occurred at work with a colleague or with research or with a patient; these challenges sometimes lead to falling into a dark, deep hole of despair. And, once more I will experience the dreaded hopelessness and helplessness that once entrapped me as a child. At first, it took me considerable time to identify the precipitants. Over time, these negative emotional periods have become fewer and their duration shorter as I've realized that I'm no longer "back there as a helpless boy"; instead, I'm here in the present with the requisite skills to resolve the issue and finally, exit the predicament.

One cannot grow up in a toxic home environment during childhood and adolescence and then be rid of all the demons, once and for all. However, the demons may be defeated as regards their long-standing affectual power to influence with their terrible constrictive prisons of emotional confinement. In short, one can learn to free oneself of the past and be liberated by practicing the new life skills to resolve difficulties; however, I remain vigilantly aware that my past is always ready to re-present itself in the form of a new stressor—sometimes at the most inopportune moment.

I close *Part One* feeling grateful for the life I've had and have now. Is my life best described as swimming upstream? I think so. Has it been difficult? Yes. But, I have to say that I've lived my life as I wanted to and achieved most of the desired outcomes I have set; more specifically, I have achieved the aims having to do with learning to self-control my personal life, realized and maintained the kind of marriage I wanted with Rosemary, been a good father to my children, Mike, John and Kristin and finally, produced a successful clinical career. Overall, and in contrast to Ivan in Dostoyevsky's *The Brothers Karamazov*, the trip has been worth it, and I'll keep the ticket.

I'm closing *Part One* with a prayer I wrote in June 2018, expressing my thoughts about my life and its history and the continuous challenges I described above.

My Lord: Thank you for another day to live. You know me so well. You know my dreams, my thoughts, my past and present—much better than I know myself. You know the barren waste-land that underlies many of my early days as a child and the contents of its aberrant influences. Every now and then, I fall into the grasp of its cauldron of hell, either through dreams or in the day's real moments. My breath is taken away with terror-filled experiences. These moments I relive in a valley of death with a companion of nothingness—feeling helpless. Even now this morning, You meet me and stand with me affirming my steps. You keep enabling me to stand upright and straight. Being the source of my courage to face existence head-on during the day is beyond my understanding. Grasp me this morning with Your Grace and let me bask in Your Presence as I try to live the day with You. Help me to meet Rosemary, my family and others with a kind and helpful heart—one that is filled with HOPE.

PART TWO:
Evolution of CBASP

Chapter Eight:

The Beginnings of CBASP

If I accomplish my goals in writing *Part Two*, I will have successfully demonstrated that the techniques of the CBASP model emerged from my struggles and from my efforts to construct a general methodology to resolve these problems as well as modify the similar problems facing the chronic patients I've treated. The structure of the various techniques of CBASP cannot be separated from my personal life dilemmas and must be understood from this perspective. I will use personal examples in the following chapters as well as utilize some case examples to help make the techniques understandable to the reader.

A Brief Mental Health History of Depression. I've treated what we call "episodic" major depression (MD) since 1971. One diagnostic criterion for MD is that patients report being continuously depressed for two consecutive weeks. Many of these adult patients describe their depression course as lasting much longer—some report a continuous course of depression beginning during early adolescence. Prior to 1981, there was no diagnostic category for chronic depression, nor was the long-term disorder considered to be treatable using either psychotherapy or medicine. Before the early 1980s, the psychiatric field believed that individuals presenting with long-term depression should be classified as a personality disorder (PD): the diagnosis should be "cyclothymic personality disorder, depressive type."

Depression research during the 1980s and beyond demonstrated that long-term depression may respond to psychotherapy and/or medicine and reminded us that we needed to rethink the assumptions about depression in general. Today, we now know there are two types of depression: episodic major depression and the long-term chronic depression which we label Persistent Depressive Disorder (PDD). The latter form lasts a minimum of two years and more often than not, the duration is much longer. There are two sources for long-term chronic depression. Approximately twenty percent of young adults who report their first major depression onset around age twenty-five will become chronically depressed. The second chronic group will report their depression began during their teens. The individuals in both groups are diagnosed, Persistent Depressive Disorder (PDD). PDD, while not as prevalent as episodic MD, describes many patients who have MD coexisting with a second long-term form of milder depression (dysthymia), a condition that lingers for years and becomes a lifetime disorder unless treated adequately.

My Early Treatment Failures. In the beginning of my practice in the early 1970s, I was making no distinction between episodic MD and PDD; instead, I was treating everyone the same. Over time, I observed that the episodic MD individuals usually improved with psychotherapy with or without medication while the chronic patients did not. I began to look more closely at why "non-response" characterized the long-term patients. I even collected research data on samples of "untreated" chronic patients who had been depressed for longer than two years.

Would they, over time, get better (remit) without any treatment? Publishing these data during the mid-1980s illustrated that less than ten percent of these individuals remitted during a one year period, and of this ten percent remitters group, one-half relapsed over the next four years. Simultaneously, depression research in the field was also demonstrating that the chronic disorder was qualitatively different in many respects when compared to the episodic type. Researchers examined onset age, history of the presence of physical abuse, emotional abuse, emotional deprivation and sexual abuse, general family history configurations, suicidality issues, psychotherapy response rates, medication response rates, comorbid psychopathology, relapse rates after treatment termination, and the waxing and waning of the course of depression over extended time periods (e.g., up to ten years). When all of these differences were statistically analyzed, the data illustrated that episodic MD and chronic depression were distinctive disorders. Another finding was that the different forms of chronic depression, and there are several, were more alike than different and all could be treated similarly.

Half of my career has been spent conducting diagnostic research with the chronic disorders. After thirty years of our research comparing episodic MD with chronic depression, my colleagues and I were finally rewarded in 2013 when the *5th Edition* of the American Psychiatric Association's manual, *Diagnostic & Statistical Manual of Mental Disorders*, made chronic depression (i.e. PDD) an independent category differentiating it from episodic MD.

Through the early 1970s before I became aware of the episodic versus chronic distinctions, I applied several popularly administered psychotherapy approaches to patients whom I recognized later were chronically depressed. I administered Roger's Non-Directive Psychotherapy, Beck's Cognitive Therapy and Ferster's Behavioral Activation approaches. I achieved little to no success. Non-response was the usual outcome since the refractory patterns of behaving, thinking and emoting remained unchanged. Thus, I went back to the drawing board and looked further at the history and symptom patterns of my patients. *All of a sudden, their history and symptom landscape began to look familiar! More often than not, I was looking at myself, my history and my long-term symptoms.* Subsequently, I asked myself what might work to free an individual who was as stuck-in-a-rut as I previously was.

So, I began to look more closely at my chronic patients and to listen more closely to the way they talked, how they expressed their perceptions of the world of others, and how self-destructive they were regardless of the obvious predictable and negative consequences they reported. They seemed to be intent on self-destructive behavior in interpersonal relationships. These hurtful interpersonal consequences had little to no effect on how they behaved. All of these patterns made no logical sense to me in the beginning. Most human beings are programmed to avoid pain—these patients were not.

As I continued to ponder this dilemma, I realized something. These patients didn't think like I did, their logic was pre-causal/pre-logical in structure and they functioned as if the only thing in their life was *me, myself and I*. Simply put, they were completely egotistical and were not influenced at all by what other people did or said. They were miserable human beings and they continued in their chronic orbit of misery unaffected by any external social influences. In fact, they were persons who had no social environment—all they had in the world were themselves. Their perceptual conclusions, as far as I could determine, mimicked that of four- to five-year-old children: *The world is the way it is because I believe it is.* Jean Piaget labeled the cognitive thinking of such individuals, *pre-operational functioning.*

Here is an example of pre-causal thinking that one of my female patients reported who attended a company picnic and wanted her picture taken.

Patient: Company photographer didn't take my picture at the company picnic. He took Susan, Jane, and Phyllis' pictures but not mine. He didn't take my picture because he doesn't like me.

Therapist: Did you ask him to take your picture?

Patient: It wouldn't have mattered. He would not have done it because he doesn't like me.

Therapist: What evidence do you have for this assumption? How do you know he doesn't like you?

Patient: I've never asked him. I don't have to. I just know he doesn't like me.

I further reasoned that traditional psychotherapy approaches were not effective because these individuals operated in an immature, childish circle of intra-personal functioning that was inaccessible to our usual more mature forms of social influence. As I thought further about their dilemma, I remembered my own interpersonal fears and helplessness-hopelessness history and how I avoided all the interpersonal attempts of others to get me to use reasoning and logic. It didn't work. Even as an adolescent and young adult, I was a "little boy" living behind a locked door, and I didn't know how to unlock it—there was no key. These chronic patients were the same: they were often developmentally train-wrecked little boys and girls, locked behind closed doors of interpersonal fear and avoidance and there was no key.

I determined to find a key.

Serendipitously, during my early career in the 1970s, an adolescent sixteen-year-old male patient was referred to me for anger-management training. He was not depressed but my subsequent treatment of Billy, though he was not my usual kind of patient, revised my entire approach to the treatment of chronic depression. It marked the turning point in the way I viewed and practiced psychotherapy with PDD patients. Briefly, here's what happened:

Billy was kicked off his high school football team for fighting with his teammates. He was a center linebacker and one of the best players on the squad. The last fight he had at practice resulted in the coach telling him that he was "off the team." He had to be physically restrained from hitting the coach. Several of the assistants took him to the principal's office; the principal subsequently suspended him from school for the third time that fall. I was called by the principal and asked if I could help Billy with anger-control training. I agreed to try and an appointment in my office was made for the next afternoon. Billy was on time and after sitting down made it clear to me that, "I can whip anyone, anytime, and anyplace." My immediate reply was, "And, what has that gotten you?" He responded, "Suspended and kicked off the team." We talked briefly, and then I enlisted his help to engage me in some role play where we would re-enact the confrontation between him and the coach. He reluctantly agreed. After he described the confrontation, I started and recorded the first role play: he played himself and I played the coach and began by telling him loudly that he was "off the team!" What followed was a series of non-verbal movements on his part like rolling his eyes back in his head, balling up his fists, tilting his spine backwards and shaking his arms. At one point, I thought he was going to hit me. I stood my ground and told him again, he was "off the team!" Then we stopped and watched the tape together. I found it easy to counter-aggress with his obvious anger expressions. What we saw caused him embarrassment and he reacted with: "I look stupid and queer." I agreed and then said, "Let's do it once more and this time, just say what you want without all your bodily antics. Just talk to me."

We role played the episode for a second time and looked at the tape. What happened was totally unplanned. As we watched the tape, I became the focus of his attention as I was shuffling my feet while he talked, and I couldn't think of what to say and mouthed a lot of "eh," "eh," "ehs." He exclaimed loudly, "You are different!" I said, "Why am I different?" He replied, "Because I was different!" And I said, "Yes, you changed my behavior by changing yours!" This led to a successful case outcome over the next few weeks. Billy had no more school suspensions or fights during a two-year follow-up period.

Demonstrating to Billy that his behavior had interpersonal consequences led me to wonder if "contingency-training" might also be a relevant approach with chronic patients. It might work because of the chronic patient's pre-causal/pre-logical way of thinking. The method I was thinking about would not be delivered through the usual verbal talk; rather, it would be administered via a behavioral demonstration with the goal being to illustrate that behavior has consequences. In a critical way, my chronic patients and Billy were similar, for both saw no connection between what they did and the consequences they produced. They were cut off from others! Remembering my earlier history also explained why some adults live with no perceived connection to the social world of others.

I remembered back to my younger days. Not only did my behavior in the present remain unaffected regardless of how others treated me - their reactions had no informing effect on what I did in the future. Earlier maltreatment had taught me to survive by living solely on an isolated island. I was unchangeable, I was unaffected by my social environment's reaction to what I did, and I remained miserable as long as I continued to live this way.

Summarily, this was Billy's personal story and, I opined strongly, the personal story of many of my chronic patients. I had overestimated the cognitive-emotive mental capability of my PDD patients. I realized further that I had been working with developmental-maturational train-wrecks (i.e. little boys and girls) who dressed in adult clothing, and this feature had been misleading and led to my overestimating their capability — they dressed like adults, they looked like adults, and I had assumed that they were, in fact, mature adults. No wonder my efforts had failed!

Constructing a New Model of Treatment. The first thing I did was to answer two questions: (1) what type of THERAPY PROCEDURE would be required to demonstrate that the patient's problems *produced specific interpersonal consequences*? And secondly, (2) what type of THERAPIST ROLE would be necessary to choreograph this contingent procedure? Said another way, if I successfully replicated the style that Dr. Hank Olivier employed in my treatment, what would a *disciplined personal involvement role* look like?

Question 1: Choreographing Behavioral Consequences. My goal was to construct a procedure that began simply and taught patients at their pace, over time, to behave, think and emote as adults. My assumption here was: I was able, with help, to mature cognitively and emotionally and so could my PDD patients. Using Billy's case as a procedural example, I constructed a method to demonstrate the maladaptive interpersonal consequences of behavior. I would no longer only talk to patients about their problems; rather, I would show them that what they did had specific consequences. This would be accomplished by first teaching them to describe specific time-limited interactions (*slices of time*) that had discernible beginning and ending points. Patients would then learn to describe what they did in these time-limited situations that led to some actual outcome. They would learn to describe the actual outcome (situational consequences) in one behavioral sentence. My thinking was if I could teach individuals to describe encounters which had specific outcomes, both of us would be able to observe, first-hand, the interpersonal effects of their behavior. Such a method, if it helped me to demonstrate behavior and its consequences, might also perceptually "connect" behavior and consequences in the minds of patients. The method would also make it difficult for individuals to deny that they had produced the consequences they had just described. Thus, I undertook the task of choreographing consequences (actual outcomes) in the session and the CBASP method was launched.

Question 2: Disciplined Personal Involvement Therapist Role. In thinking back over the role others had played in the positive life changes I made over the years, I thought back to Dr. Henry Olivier, the Binkley Boys, Rosemary and Bill Boardman and how the authentic style of being oneself had resulted in my being able to achieve salubrious attachments and learn to live adaptively. The therapy model I was considering must also actualize the therapist role in an authentic and personally-involved manner. The role must be framed from an interpersonal perspective with the patient's well-being the first priority and clinicians applying the contingent methodology in a "disciplined" manner. More will be said about the word "disciplined" in *Chapter Nine*.

Chapter Nine:

Disciplined Personal Involvement (DPI)

The CBASP's therapist role is labeled, *Disciplined Personal Involvement* (DPI), and the way clinicians administer this role becomes the launching pad to achieve the first goal of CBASP - —that is, the creation of *safety within the therapy relationship (i.e. dyadic safety)*. Patients who have been maltreated as children, as I described in my history in *Part One*, frequently enter treatment interpersonally detached, withdrawn and fearful of interactions. Clinicians who remain interpersonally inaccessible employing a traditional "professional stance" and who stand behind walls of professional anonymity and non-involvement will not likely facilitate interpersonal behavior change with such patients. The disciplined personal involvement role denotes a willingness to "be a comrade" to an individual who, more than likely, never had one. Distrust and fear of interpersonal relationship, not trust, is the dominant patient reaction to other people.

Since the creation of relational safety requires time, therapists must proceed slowly in treatment and move with an awareness of the difficulty that patients associate with interpersonal relationship. I remember how my silences in the beginning sessions with Dr. Olivier became increasingly uncomfortable. Hank waited patiently for me to talk. Obviously, he knew I was struggling over what to say and he was right, I didn't know where to begin. I was thinking about pleasing him with what I said and not thinking about what I wanted to say. Putting the patient's well-being first is the cardinal rule of DPI.

I did learn over time that I was not there to meet Dr. Olivier's emotional needs and please him by saying the 'right thing.' Once I began to talk about myself, he responded but always with my issues being his primary focus. Because his rejection of me never occurred, it took time, but I finally realized that with him I was in an *interpersonal safety-zone*—a zone where being honest and being myself were acceptable. The stronger I became psychologically, the more forthcoming and reactive he became. His comments included both positive and negative reactions. When I was off-base and hiding while blaming someone else for my foibles, he didn't hesitate to expose my flight from responsibility. For example, "Did you think that what you said may have caused his reaction?" When I reported doing something laudatory, he responded quickly and approvingly: "You did well in that situation." I learned over time that I was working with a comrade, someone who was walking with me and treating me with honest respect.

A Touchstone for Normalcy. It mattered a great deal to me what Hank thought of me as a person as well as what he thought about what I did. His responses began to influence my behavior in normal directions. With him and because of his verbal and nonverbal behaviors toward me, I was learning how to be a "normal" human being. This is a core assumption of the DPI role in the CBASP model: *Chronic patients enter CBASP psychotherapy to learn from their therapists how to behave adaptively, authentically and empathically.*

This assumption, as I've tried to illustrate above, is critical because most PDD patients have never learned the basic mechanics of positive social interaction; their long-standing fears and relational avoidance have severely compromised this learning and precluded the acquisition of basic social skills. In short, the most effective CBASP therapists, while working with patients over time, teach them to be normal human beings by becoming trusted comrades. Social skill learning may sometimes be so rudimentary that one feels silly not having acquired it earlier; and it can only be acquired in an interpersonal arena of felt-safety when patients can let down their guards and be honest.

It's also not unusual for chronic patients to admit they haven't previously experienced interpersonal trust. Traditionally trained clinicians are often perplexed when faced with patients who lack the ability to generate interpersonal trust. Letting down the traditional professional barriers and becoming an authentic human being in the therapy room is a requisite maneuver to help patients generate trust. Over the years I've found it easy to address this issue because I'm not hesitant to admit that I had the same difficulty. The patient's first question is always: "How did you do it?" My response is usually that I encountered people around whom I could admit my difficulty. Then, when no rejection followed and I felt safe, I learned over time that these persons were trustworthy and a new interpersonal day dawned for me.

Becoming an "authentic" practitioner using DPI is only learned through intense training and supervision. The didactic process more often than not involves un-learning many "professionally trained" behaviors that maintain interpersonal distance. Then, these habits are replaced with reciprocally interactive patterns. I must also caution that I do not advocate using DPI with patients who do not present with chronic depression. DPI has been devised to address the particular idiosyncratic features of the chronic patient. It is not a universal practice I administer for all types of patients.

Personal Discipline is the Key. The word "discipline" is the key term here. More time in CBASP supervision is spent teaching DPI behavior than is spent in other CBASP training areas. As emphasized above, clinicians must learn to administer DPI so that their dyadic reactions are *always* delivered with the well-being of the patient in mind. What does this mean? It means that these reactions involve the verbal articulation of the restricted feelings, attitudes and thoughts therapists are experiencing because of the patient's behavior (e.g., the inhibitive thought leading me to assume in traditional psychotherapy, that "I can't say this or the patient will think I'm negatively judging him;" versus, overtly asking the patient in a DPI manner, "Why are you treating me this way?"). DPI reactions also include instances when therapists express caring feelings for patients who need to hear it. Statements may express acceptance, respect, and concern to individuals as when therapists verbalize pride and joy over what an emotionally deprived or neglected patient has done (e.g., "I'm delighted about what you just told me you did!"). In other contexts, practitioners who may want to emphasize intense emotional reactions concerning the hurtful behavior of significant others, might exclaim: "What you told me your stepfather did to you makes me want to puke!"

In summary, many chronic patients present severely damaged developmental, cognitive-emotional and behavioral histories. This was my lot when I began working with Dr. Olivier. CBASP therapists treat primitive-functioning adults. In the beginning, they behave cognitively and emotionally like "little boys and girls;" however, these immature individuals have the capacity to grow and mature within a DPI relationship. The role assumes this growth potential and gives therapists permission to be disciplined, authentic persons who are personally involved with patients. The role also encourages practitioners to behave in the sessions as interpersonal partners where felt-safety, interpersonal trust, mature-normal functioning and problem-solving skills are experienced and acquired.

In the second session, the Significant Other History (SOH) is administered. *Chapter Ten* describes this procedure.

Chapter Ten:

The Significant Other History (SOH)

Just as my parents had been Significant Others (SOs) for me and influenced my life in momentous ways, I realized that my patients had similar informing SOs. I developed the Significant Other History to elicit this information in order to identify the early abuse and the key SOs who administered it.

Drawing from my early experiences, I hypothesized that developmental patterns of abuse translate into patient expectancies about what is likely to happen in psychotherapy; these expectancies often create the interpersonal dangers that lurk in the therapist-patient relationship. Being able to pinpoint the injurious expectancies and the individuals who taught patients to anticipate the negative outcomes is the goal of the Significant Other History procedure (SOH). Using the SOH information equips therapists to prepare for these potholes and relational landmines. Those clinicians who plunge into treatment with PDD patients and who remain unaware of the contributing factors that lead to chronic depression often confront unexpected interpersonal obstacles that easily rupture, sometimes fatally, the therapeutic relationship.

During the second session, the *core interpersonal fears* of the patient are identified with the Significant Other History (SOH). Patients often enter treatment fearing specific negative reactions from therapists when they behave in certain ways. Some fears they are aware of, others remain out-of-awareness. The SOH, an interpersonal-emotional history-taking assessment procedure, pinpoints these fearful-expectancies that may occur in four interpersonal domains. These domains represent events that happen in almost all psychotherapies. The domains are as follows: (1) *relational intimacy* between the patient and therapist; (2) the patient's *behavioral disclosures* of highly personal content material; (3) patients make *mistakes* during treatment; and (4) patients *feel or express negative emotions* toward the therapist.

At the end of session one, the patient is asked to come to the next session with a list of five to six significant others. The SOs are the "major players" in the patient's life, persons who have influenced the individual to be who they are or informed their life's direction. Once the list is written out on a flip chart, the therapist reviews the list one-by-one and requests two pieces of information for each significant other: (1) recall several memories you have interacting with this individual; and, (2) pinpoint one "stamp," or "legacy of influence" the person left with you. Stamps or legacies are usually the negative consequences patients received from a malevolent significant other at an earlier time (e.g., "*When* I said or did this, *then* the negative consequence occurred," etc.). Stamps/legacies also denote the fear-expectancies patients bring to treatment along with the consequences they expect to occur when the same type of event (i.e. closeness, disclosures, mistakes and negatively expressed emotions) happens in therapy. The expectancy is that their clinician will react just like hurtful significant others did.

The two-step SOH procedure is administered with each listed significant other until the entire list is covered. At this point, the clinician and patient then review the "stamp" for each SO and look for any consistent fear-avoidant theme(s) within the list of stamps that might point to one of the four interpersonal domains. For example, would there be a negative rejection-expectancy present if a "relational intimacy" moment occurred (e.g., "If I get close to Dr. Smith, then he will reject me.")? If the person disclosed "personal-intimate" content, what is the fear-expectancy (e.g., "If I share something that I've never told anyone, Dr. Jones will ridicule me.")? Or thirdly, if a patient "makes a mistake" during treatment, what's the fear? (e.g., "If I was late for an appointment/ forgot an appointment, then Dr. Samuels would not want to see me anymore."); and finally, if patients became "frustrated" or "angry" with therapists, would rejection or censure accompany the expressed emotion (e.g., "If I told Dr. Phillips that I'm angry with her, then she would reject me.")?

Further examples of learned fear-avoidant expectancies that I have obtained from SOH administrations and that have become materials for my transference hypothesis constructions are shown below in the following verbatim scenarios:

1. Therapist: Have you ever trusted anyone before?

   Patient (24-year-old female depressed for 12 years): Everyone I've known has hurt me or at least tried. [*Interpersonal Intimacy*]

   Transference Hypothesis: If I get close to Dr. McCullough, then he will hurt/reject me.

2. Therapist: Have you ever had a successful relationship?

Patient (57-yr-old female depressed for 45 years): No. I've screwed up every relationship I've ever had with my mistakes, —even my last marriage. [*Making Mistakes*]

Transference Hypothesis: If I make a mistake with Dr. McCullough, then he will end the relationship with me.

3. Therapist: If you and I work together, what do you expect will happen?

Patient (35-yr-old male depressed for 17 years): Nothing. I don't expect to get anything out of my work with you. [*Interpersonal Intimacy issue stemming from an emotional deprivation history*]

Transference Hypothesis: If I work with Dr. McCullough, this endeavor will do nothing for me; —it will add nothing to my life.

Thinking back on my work with Dr. Olivier, I was fearful in three of the interpersonal domains. I was not afraid to express anger. Chief among the three that did evoke noteworthy fear-avoidant expectancies was the *relational intimacy area*. I was afraid of the danger of feeling close to Hank and of what might happen in intimate or close moments. I had no idea what I would do if this happened.

CBASP therapists, after reviewing all the stamps from the SO list, designate one core-fear domain as being the most salient. Next, the practitioner constructs a one-sentence *Transference Hypothesis* (TH) making explicit the patient's core-fear and what consequence would follow if this fear event occurred in the session. For example, if Hank had rated the "relational intimacy" domain as the most salient core-fear domain for me, then he would have constructed the following TH on me: "If Jim gets interpersonally close to me [core-fear event], then I will begin to point out Jim's mistakes and weaknesses and tell him what a loser he is" [expected consequences]. This TH would have been derived from my SOH material that included "father" memories [i.e. what it was like growing up with my father: *the core-fear event*] and the corresponding consequence or stamp [i.e. getting close to my father resulted in getting hurt: *the expected consequence*].

Whenever Hank and I experienced moments of relational closeness, we entered a "hot spot" territory. Hank could have used his TH on me in these hot spot moments to teach me to discriminate between closeness with my father and closeness with him where there would be no rejection or punishment. The interpersonal goal in identifying fear-avoidant moments (i.e. the 'hot spot' as identified by the TH) is to facilitate one to make appropriate emotional discriminations. The TH is employed as a vehicle to create a "safety zone" between therapist and patient. Safety is realized when patients can accurately discriminate between the ways hurtful significant others reacted and the positive responses of the practitioner. We move now to the next chapter where I show how the *Interpersonal Discrimination Exercise* (IDE) uses the TH to help patients make these safety discriminations.

Chapter Eleven:

Interpersonal Discrimination Exercise and the Creation of Felt Safety

I designed the Interpersonal Discrimination Exercise (IDE) to interrupt the orbit of sameness which entraps the chronic patient, and it is administered in approximately thirty percent of the sessions. As noted before and from the patient's point of view, today's malevolence is a replay of the experiences in the past and the future predicts only more rejection and hurt. At the outset of treatment, this orbit of sameness plays out in the therapy room, where the clinician is mistakenly perceived as being no different from maltreating significant others; that is, the patient expects that the clinician will treat her the way she has been treated previously. Practitioners interrupt or break into this orbit of sameness with the IDE by requiring the patient to make an accurate discrimination between the patient's hurtful SOs and the therapist. Put in more literal terms, what is taught the patient in the IDE is to revise their misperceived identity of the psychotherapist: For example, *"I'm not your mother!" "I'm not your father!" "I'm not your sister or your brother!" "I'm not your uncle or your aunt!" "I'm not your minister!" "I'm*

not a neighbor!" "I'm not anyone who has hurt you in the past- —I'm differ-
ent. I'm someone else, and I will not treat you as you have been treated!" "Deal
with me in terms of who I really am!"

I wish I could accurately recall how long it took me to stop constructing
Dr. Olivier into persons he was not and reacting to him, cognitively
and emotionally, in ways that were inappropriate. I do remember that
it took a while. I behaved toward him as if he were my father, my
mother and other individuals who had hurt me in the past, and I expected him to react to me as they had. These cognitive-emotional dis-
tortions or transfer-of-learning errors were very difficult to correct and
the remediation process took a long time.

Such learning is indeed challenging and literally requires repeated IDE
learning trials. It cannot be achieved in one administration of the IDE.
These erroneous perceptions are so entrenched in the brain's "granite
memory system" that in 2000 I wrote a description of what modifying
them is like:

Treating the chronically depressed adult, dislodging the refractory cognitive-emotional and behavioral armor that is the disorder, is analogous
to breaking through a granite wall using a ten-pound sledgehammer.
One hits the wall repeatedly in the same area with little or no effect
until, almost imperceptibly, a slight hairline crack appears. Under continuous pounding, the crack gradually enlarges until, finally, the wall
breaks and crumbles.

The IDE is a proactive approach and uses the transference hypothesis
at times when the TH is implicated in a hot spot domain. The following
scenario demonstrates the four steps that are employed. I'll demonstrate by using our standard example of me and Dr. Olivier with the
transference hypothesis being the same as the one Hank constructed
earlier on me: "If Jim gets interpersonally close to me [core-fear event],

then I will begin to point out Jim's mistakes and weaknesses and tell him what a loser he is" [expected consequences]. The hot spot situation occurred in the eighth session when Hank gently expressed his regret that I had received such a stern and cutting rebuke from my father. He did it in an obvious, sincere and tender manner. Subsequently, I thanked him and was unexpectedly surprised he reacted this way. The hot spot was obvious as the relational closeness moment was present (and Hank knew it). Here's how he would have administered the IDE:

(1) Dr. Olivier: "If you had told your father about being sternly rebuked by someone, how would he have reacted?"

Jim: He would have said something like, "You should be able to be tough and not be bothered by what others say."

Dr. Olivier: "How would your mother have reacted had you told her what had happened?"

Jim: She might have said, "That's too bad. He was wrong to do that."

(2) Dr. Olivier: "Now Jim, I want you to carefully think about this before you answer. How did I react to you when you told me about the stern rebuke?"

Jim: "You didn't say much."

Dr. Olivier: "Think again. What was my facial expression like? How did my voice sound and what exactly did I say?"

Jim: "Well, you did talk lower, and you sounded like you felt bad for me."

Dr. Olivier: "You're right. What else did I do?"

Jim: "Come to think of it now, you sounded like you were on my side and were sorry about what had happened to me. It made me feel good inside that you were affected that way."

(3) Dr. Olivier: "Now, you are observing correctly what I did and said and you're also picking up on the fact that I am on your side and care what happens to you. I want to ask you to do something else for me. Compare and contrast your father and mother's reactions and my reaction - —how are they alike and different?"

Jim: "There's no similarity between your reaction and my father's. My mother's reaction was okay but she quickly judged the other person to be in the wrong. It didn't have much effect on me. Your reaction, on the other hand, made me feel better, and I felt that you were in my court and had my back. Your reaction was quite different compared to theirs."

(4) Dr. Olivier: "I've got one more request. What if in our work together, you really conclude that I am really different compared to your father and mother. What possibilities open up for US if I really turn out to be different compared to your parents?"

Jim: "At this point, I'm not real sure. But it surely feels different right now."

These are the four-steps in the exercise: (1) First, Hank, using his TH on me, focused my attention on a specific relational intimacy moment involving his response to my story about my father. To initiate the interpersonal discrimination process, he asked me how my father would have reacted had I told him about some similar event that had happened;

(2) next, he asked me how he had reacted to my description of what happened; (3) thirdly, I was requested to compare and contrast his response with that of my two SOs; and (4) finally, he asked me to describe the implications for US if I finally concluded that he, in fact, *was* different and *would* respond differently compared to what I had experienced in the past. Summarily, the IDE emphasizes that this is the way it was for you in the PAST, and this is the way things are for you in the PRESENT, with me, your therapist! Relational safety was actualized to the degree that I came to realize that Dr. Olivier was not my father or mother. Then, I had to learn to relate to him interpersonally in terms of who he really was.

Core-fears obscure interpersonal realities and preclude one from dealing with others in accurate ways. In *Part One*, I described how I concluded that, as a child, I was entrapped in a 'no exit,' unchanging environment of abuse and harm. Not only did I have no answer for resolving the negative state of affairs between myself and my parents, but also I couldn't conceive of living any other way. This view was the only reality I knew, so without actually being aware of it, I thought that the way things were in my family was just the way life was - —period...... end of story... and finis! I lived with this dominating perception of reality for many years. Were these interpersonal perceptions, beliefs and assumptions fallacious? Many would reply with a loud, "Yes!" However, the irony is that in reality they were not fallacious assumptions for me. They were valid perceptions of the only reality I knew at the time.

Hank was wise enough to know that cognitive persuasion techniques would not have worked with me; that is, he knew that he could not intellectually convince me that the way I saw life was erroneous because he knew that maltreatment was the only reality that I had known. He also knew that until I had other interpersonal experiences that countered these hard-wired connections in my brain, I would remain stuck in a rut. *Thus, in his treatment, he set out to become an interpersonal alternative that counter-challenged my reality views.* He achieved his treatment goal over time by focusing my attention on the differences that existed between him and the hurtful others.

The "key to my door of freedom" was my relationship with him and I acquired the learned discrimination that our relationship differed qualitatively from previous significant other relationships. Said another way, the outcome of our work was that I perceived my present as being qualitatively different from my malevolent past and my future was open-ended. Interpersonal safety had replaced the fear-avoidance that had dominated my life for so long.

Chapter Twelve:

Situational Analysis Exercise

Situational Analysis (SA) is an in-session demonstration exercise that highlights the behavioral problems of the patient and the consequences that accrue. It makes patient problems explicit and shows chronic depressives how they create and produce their own self-destructive outcomes.

SA was developed from my earlier experiences with Billy whom I introduced in *Chapter Eight*. In the beginning of treatment, most chronic patients do not understand that they produce the misery they complain of because they are not social-interpersonal abstract thinkers. Today, research tells us that non-abstract adult thinkers can be coached to think abstractly. The repeated use of SA will help them to think abstractly and change their lives.

Mismatching Demands of SA. SA is also categorized as a "mismatching demands" exercise. When non-abstractive thinking individuals master the SA task, they learn to use the intellectual skills required to think on a plane exceeding their primitive developmental level. Their cognitive operations or level of thinking will be sufficiently challenged in SA and maturation-cognitive shifts will follow. How this is accomplished will become clearer in a moment.

Teaching preoperational patients to solve interpersonal problems on a formal (abstract) level results in a structural reorganization of thinking and emotion. Patients are moved to a more mature level of cognitive-emotional functioning. SA is a central technique of CBASP and achieves the second major goal of CBASP [the first goal being *relational safety*] which is *perceptually connecting patients to the social world they live in* by teaching them to recognize the consequences of their behavior.

Readers may be asking themselves these questions: How does one begin in the early sessions with a pre-causal thinking "adult-child" and teach them to function like a mature individual? How does one teach a person who only thinks in a global manner (e.g., "No one likes me." "Nothing will ever work out for me." "I'll never succeed." etc.) to focus on specific problems and learn to solve them? How does one teach a patient to think of others and generate empathy? How does one approach the felt helplessness and hopelessness dilemma of the chronic patient and replace these debilitating emotions with feelings of empowerment? How does one perceptually connect the fearful-avoidant patient with the social world of others when they have been interpersonally avoidant for years? The above challenges are resolved with SA, which is administered repeatedly in approximately seventy percent of the CBASP sessions.

SA Methodology. In SA, patients learn to describe one situational event [*an arbitrary slice of time*] that occurred between the patient and another person (Situational Description). Then, they formulate one to three interpretations that reflect the intrapersonal meaning the encounter (Interpretations) had for the patient. Next, they express how they behaved in the situation (i.e. the tone of their voice, their non-verbal expressions, the words they used, etc.). Fourthly, patients describe the Actual Outcome or how the situation turned out for them [*i.e. the consequences of their behavior in the situation*]. The fifth step has patients state in one sentence, how they would have liked the situation to have turned out (i.e. the Desired Outcome). The Desired Outcome becomes the *situational goal* and *motivational component of the exercise.*

Desired Outcomes (DOs) are rarely achieved in early SA administrations; rather, mismanaging interpersonal situations and not achieving one's Desired Outcome are usually the norm and this is made explicit in the exercise. Patients, in being bound by the slice of time situation, are not allowed to move into global thinking (e.g., "No one likes me." "Nothing will ever work out for me."); instead, they must remain focused on what happened in the situational slice of time and confront the cognitive and behavioral errors that resulted in a poor Actual Outcome (AO) - one that was not equivalent to their Desired Outcome. Said another way, they didn't get what they wanted when the AO ≠ DO. Having to confront the consequences of one's behavior, particularly when the consequences are not desirable, is usually an experience the patient has never encountered before. It's anxiety evoking but sets the motivational wheels in motion for change. SA leaves the burden of change in the patient's court. If they want to achieve their Desired Outcomes, they will have to change their behavior. If nothing changes, their Desired Outcomes remain unrealized.

Over time, patients learn to concentrate on the small "slice of time" by using abstractive thought. They must think *about* alternatives. They must think *about* what they want. They must think *about others* in realistic ways. They must *evaluate* their problem solving efficacy and *correct* their mistakes. As patients move toward mastery of SA, they use abstractive thought. They look at themselves, others and their social world in alternative ways. The upshot is that interpersonal possibilities now open up and are seriously considered, countering the old negative thinking [i.e. *the way it is, is the way it has to be*].

Disciplined Personal Involvement. Psychotherapists teach patients how to master the SA methodology through repeated practice over sessions. The role of the teacher here is critical. The patient works with a thoughtful comrade who provides constant feedback and who also applauds successful mastery of each step. SA administration relies heavily on the disciplined personal involvement role, and the role is informed by the transference hypothesis (TH) which has previously identified the core-fear. TH "hot spots" occur frequently during these exercises. Depending on where the TH domain lies, clinicians are sensitive to these particular areas when they teach SA. For example, if the core-fear lies in the *relational intimacy domain* where past rejection has been present, teaching is delivered without censure or rejection. If the patient reports that *personal mistakes* have led to punitive reactions by SOs, encouragement and gentle correction must replace the expected hostile feedback. Whenever a "hot spot" moment occurs during the procedure, the Interpersonal Discrimination Exercise is administered following the SA exercise. The behavior of the clinician in the situational context, as it pertains to the TH, is compared to that of maltreating SOs. Interpersonal discrimination feedback in the IDE begins early in treatment and continues throughout.

During the early sessions, patients are frequently reminded to stay on task (i.e. within the slice of time) and proceed through the steps until they formulate a Desired Outcome. Conceptualizing the Desired Outcome is an abstractive task that, at first, is often a difficult step for many. Not only have patients not previously considered what they wanted, but more than likely, they have never considered producing a positive Actual Outcome with another individual. SA walks patients through an abstractive learning task and moves them towards a desirable interpersonal goal. Then, in the first walk-through, patients and therapists review the steps to see if patients achieved their Desired Outcome [i.e. Elicitation Phase]. If the Desired Outcome was not achieved, the patient and therapist review the patient's cognitive interpretations and behaviors in a second walk-through and fix the cognitive or behavioral problems that prevented the achievement of the Desired Outcome [i.e. Remediation Phase]. The elicitation and remediation phases are conducted slowly and at the patient's learning pace. Over time, patients become adroit problem-solvers using SA, and they learn to self-administer the exercise with no assistance from the clinician.

Coincidentally, and while writing this chapter, I received an email from an individual living in the northwestern part of our country. The message disclosed a story that I've heard hundreds of times. It was the email writer's life history with chronic depression, coupled with helplessness and hopelessness. If successful therapy is achieved, he will have to be taught SA in order to produce his Desired Outcomes with others. Right now, he is stuck in a rut with himself and feeling considerable despair:

"I am 39 years old and currently on anti-depressants. Most of my life, I have had a serious, long-term history of major depression. I have done tons of psychotherapy, but it was useless, and I've never been on anti-depressants for an extended time before now. Nothing has helped. Do you know if there is anything I can do with my depression? I am at my wit's end over what to do and don't know where to turn."

Two SA Examples. Two SA examples on another patient will be presented below. The patient was a thirty-eight-year old male who had been depressed since he was ten years old. He began treatment in a major depression and complained that nothing would ever help him get rid of his depression. The first SA will illustrate his attempt at doing SA during the fourth session;—the Desired Outcome was not achieved.

The second example will show the same patient's mastery of SA during the twenty-seventh session when he obtain his Desired Outcome.

<u>Example 1</u>: Therapist is writing the SA on a flip chart in full view of the patient.

[Elicitation Phase]

Therapist: Tell me what happened?

Patient: I went to my boss' office to ask him for a raise. I'd been working on a big project for the past six months that led to a significant financial gain for our company. I felt my work merited a raise. I walked in and stood before his desk. He never looked up and asked me what I wanted. I fumbled around with what to say and finally said something like, "I wanted to ask you something." He said, "What do you want?" I said, "I need a raise." He never looked up and said, "No one is getting a raise this year." *I said nothing else, turned around and left his office. [Actual Outcome]*

Therapist: Tell me what the situation meant to you. What were you thinking in this slice of time? Use just one sentence for each interpretation.

Patient: (1) I never get anything from anyone.

Therapist: Did it mean anything else?

Patient: (2) My boss doesn't like me.

Therapist: Let's take one more interpretation before we move on.

Patient: (3) I never told him why I wanted a raise.

Therapist: Tell me how you behaved in the situation. How did you talk and stand while asking for a raise?

Patient: I think my voice was very soft, and I talked in more of a pleading manner as I think back on it. I never looked at him though I could tell he never looked up at me while I stood before him.

Therapist: I've got a good idea how you behaved and talked. Tell me how the event came out for you. What was the Actual Outcome? Look at the endpoint in your situational description. What happened at the end?

Patient: I quit talking, couldn't think of anything to say, turned around and walked out of his office.

Therapist: Now, think back on this event. How did you want the event to come out for you? What was your Desired Outcome?

Patient: I wanted to tell what I had done on the special project, and then say that I think I deserved a raise.

Therapist: Did you get what you wanted here?

Patient: No.

Therapist: Why not?

Patient: Because I'm a failure.

[Remediation Phase]

Therapist: Let's walk back through this situational event keeping the Desired Outcome in mind and see if we can "fix" the thinking and behaving parts that might have prevented you from saying to your boss:

"I want to tell you what I have done on the special project, and I think I deserve a raise."

Let's look first at the way you interpreted the situation. What was your first interpretation in this event? Look at the flip chart.

Patient: (1) I never get anything from anyone.

Therapist: Thinking this way, how does it contribute to saying what you want?

Patient: It doesn't.

Therapist: It's a global thought—not anchored in the situation. Doesn't help you at all to say what you want. What's your second interpretation?

Patient: (2) My boss doesn't like me.

Therapist: How does this interpretation contribute to you asking for a merited raise?

Patient: It doesn't.

Therapist: No, again it doesn't. We call this a 'mind read' and it's usually ineffective when you try to read another person's mind. What's your third read?

Patient: (3) I never told him why I wanted a raise.

Therapist: How did interpreting the situation like this contribute to your getting your Desired Outcome?

Patient: Well, it's true. I didn't tell him why I was asking for a raise!

Therapist: You're dang right – it's true! It's a wonderful interpretation and a clear thought that you've left something out. Now, let me introduce you to another type of interpretation or read you can use. You need something you can say to yourself in situations like this. We call it an *Action Read* - a thought that prompts you to say or do something that's needed in the moment. What could you say to yourself here that would help you obtain your Desired Outcome?

Patient: Speak up!

Therapist: Terrific. Now, had you thought this to yourself in that situation, what would you have added to your behavior? Look at your Desired Outcome on the flip chart. Tell me what you would have said?

Patient: I would have said why I came to see him: "I want to tell you what I have done on the special project, and I think I deserve a raise."

Therapist: And had you said this would you have gotten your Desired Outcome?

Patient: Yes!

Therapist: What have you learned in this SA?

Patient: I've got to focus more on what I want, and I've got to learn to speak up.

Example 2: It's the twenty-seventh session and the patient himself is writing his SA on a flip chart in full view of the therapist.

[Elicitation Phase]

Patient: Let me tell you what happened. My boss called me into his office and asked me to head up another large project for the company. I replied that I would take the project on one condition. He asked what that was, and I said that at the end of the project that I wanted a merit raise. He reacted and said that he would raise my salary by one-quarter at the termination of the project. I agreed to head up the project.

I only had one interpretation and that was to tell him my conditions for taking the project on.

Therapist: Sounds like an Action Read.

Patient: It was. The situation ended with my agreeing to take the project and his agreement that when the project was over, he would increase my salary by one-quarter. I got my Desired Outcome because I looked him right in the eye and told him exactly what I wanted.

Therapist: You cannot do any better than this! Perfect execution of this analysis! [Therapist stands up at this point and claps at the patient's obvious success]

Comparing the two SAs illustrates several significant differences: In the second SA (1) the patient is taking the initiative and has learned the SA method to criterion; (2) the therapist says little except at the end when he provides his "congratulations and applause;" (3) the patient formulated a Desired Outcome at the beginning of the encounter, and his goal directed all his behaviors in the situation; (4) there is an absence of helplessness and hopelessness in his situational report; and (5) the behavioral fear-avoidance that characterized his functioning at the beginning of treatment is gone - it has been replaced by assertion and goal-directed behavior; and (6) No *Remediation Phase* in this SA was needed as the patient got what he wanted and there were no SA step-mistakes.

Chapter Thirteen:

Epilogue

A brilliant clinical psychologist, Dr. Katherine Schaefer-Berg, revised what John Bowlby wrote when she summarized what she thought was happening in successful CBASP Psychotherapy. When patients begin treatment functioning on a primitive cognitive-emotional level and then exit therapy having learned to live as mature adults, she opined:

"New attachments in later life may lead to psychological modifications *if* the new attachments are accompanied by the development of formal operational or abstractive thought in the interpersonal domain."

Dr. Schaefer-Berg's description of the efficacy dynamics of CBASP captured the transition I began to make during young adulthood and summarized well my story about becoming human. *New interpersonal attachments* challenged my old ways of living and my isolated-living lifestyle was modified. The *"nothing will ever be different"* perception of my life gave way to abstractive social-interpersonal thinking and opened me to future cognitive-emotional possibilities. Said another way, having learned new and facilitative social skills via novel and loving attachments gave me the strength and courage to try new experiences in living.

Summarily, I learned that safe interpersonal encounter was possible with all its riches and gifts, and finally, I realized the extent to which my behavior had consequences and just how connected I was to the world I lived in. Being human requires both experiences.